ablished
l brands,
n travel.

For more than 135 years our
guidebooks have unlocked the secrets
of destinations around the world,
sharing with travellers a wealth of
experience and a passion for travel.

**Rely on Thomas Cook as your
travelling companion on your next trip
and benefit from our unique heritage.**

Thomas Cook **pocket** guides

GRANADA

Written by Nicholas Inman, updated by Josephine Quintero

Published by Thomas Cook Publishing
A division of Thomas Cook Tour Operations Limited
Company registration no. 3772199 England
The Thomas Cook Business Park, Unit 9, Coningsby Road,
Peterborough PE3 8SB, United Kingdom
Email: books@thomascook.com, Tel: +44 (0) 1733 416477
www.thomascookpublishing.com

Produced by Cambridge Publishing Management Limited
Burr Elm Court, Main Street, Caldecote CB23 7NU
www.cambridgepm.co.uk

ISBN: 978-1-84848-438-2

© 2007, 2009 Thomas Cook Publishing
This third edition © 2011
Text © Thomas Cook Publishing
Maps © Thomas Cook Publishing/PCGraphics (UK) Limited
Transport map © Communicarta Limited

Series Editor: Karen Beaulah
Production/DTP: Steven Collins

Printed and bound in Spain by GraphyCems

Cover photography © Jeremy Horner/Corbis

CONTENTS

SYMBOLS KEY

The following symbols are used throughout this book:

ⓐ address ⓣ telephone ⓦ website address ⓛ opening times
ⓝ public transport connections ❶ important

The following symbols are used on the maps:

_i_	information office	▓	point of interest
✈	airport	◯	city
✚	hospital	○	large town
⛊	police station	○	small town
🚌	bus station	—	main road
🚆	railway station		minor road
✝	cathedral	—	railway
❶	numbers denote featured cafés & restaurants	...	regional border

Hotels and restaurants are graded by approximate price as follows:
£ budget price **££** mid-range price **£££** expensive

▶ _The spectacular setting of the Alhambra_

INTRODUCING
Granada

Introduction

'Granada: the land I've dreamt of ...' run the words of a famous song, and indeed this southern Spanish city is and always has been the stuff of people's dreams. Situated at the foot of the highest mountain range in the Iberian peninsula, the Sierra Nevada ('Snowy Mountains'), which forms a constant backdrop, Granada is most visited for its Moorish heritage: the exotic art and architecture of medieval Europe's great Muslim civilisation. No one comes to Granada without seeing, in particular, the incomparable fortress-palace of the Alhambra, which is almost overwhelming in the magnificence of its interior decoration; however many Wonders of the World there really are, it's definitely one of them!

Below the Alhambra is a busy city of a quarter of a million people. A sizeable percentage of the population is made up of university students and other young people, and this happy age-imbalance has encouraged a convivial, easy-going bar-hopping culture that is another of Granada's key attractions. Most bars in the city lay on a complementary tapa (snack) with each drink you order, and serendipitously eating your way around the city in the company of friends can easily become addictive.

Another great thing about Granada is its compactness. It is a smallish city that positively encourages you to explore on foot. There is virtually no monument, museum, shop or bar of significance that you have to take public transport to get to – although it's always an option.

Being small makes Granada easy to get into and just as easy to get out of. A short series of hairpin bends south takes you up to

Europe's southernmost ski station. Alternatively, the Mediterranean beaches of the so-called 'Tropical Coast' are less than an hour away. Between the mountain tops and the seashore are the verdant valleys of the Alpujarras, which make good country for hiking or simply chilling out.

🔺 *Granada's heraldic device – the pomegranate – is a ubiquitous adornment*

When to go

SEASONS & CLIMATE

Granada has an essentially continental climate with strong contrasts between seasons, which are heavily influenced by its altitude (685 m/2,247 ft). The average annual temperature is a cool 14.8°C (58.6°F). January has a typical temperature of 6°C (43°F), but daytime temperatures can sometimes be as high as 20°C (68°F). August has a typical temperature of 25°C (77°F), but it can climb to a stifling 40°C (104°F). July and August are peak tourist months, but they can be unbearably hot. Many local people choose to decamp for the height of the summer. Autumn is a short season, but a good time to visit if you are prepared to risk some rain. Almost all the year's rain falls between October and May.

Winters can be cold but also sunny – you'll need heating to sit still in a room, but the sun, when it shines, is warm enough to have a coffee out of doors on most days of the year.

Spring comes early, this being southern Spain, and, although there may be bad weather still ahead, the weeks from late March to early June can usually be counted on for mild weather to go with a prodigious growth of flowers in parks and gardens before the heat of the summer takes hold.

ANNUAL EVENTS

There are three traditional fiestas especially worth seeing in Granada: Easter Week, the Crosses of May and the Corpus Christi fair. The ceremony to commemorate the conquest of Granada is also interesting. Any fiesta means free entertainment, but don't

🔺 *Gypsy culture forms an integral part of Granadino life*

expect a quiet night's sleep or an easy day's sightseeing. Streets may be blocked off to allow processions to pass; some monuments may be closed; and bars and restaurants are likely to be overflowing with customers.

January
Fiesta de la Toma (Commemoration of the Conquest of Granada) To celebrate the handing over of the Alhambra by its Muslim rulers to the Christians, a civic-religious ceremony is held with a procession from the Capilla Real to the town hall. Here, the youngest member of the city council theatrically waves the banner of the victorious kingdom of Castile.

March/April
Semana Santa (Easter Week) Every city in Spain holds processions for Easter Week but no other city can provide a backdrop for the lines of hooded penitents to beat the floodlit silhouette of the Alhambra. There are processions from Palm Sunday to Easter Sunday. Each one takes its own route – those to the Albaicín and Sacromonte are particularly worth seeing – but they are all funnelled into the official route at the end, which goes down Calle Navas, Plaza del Carmen, Calle Reyes Católicos, Calle Mesones, Calle Marqués de Gerona, Plaza de las Pasiegas and ends at the cathedral. On the night of Maundy Thursday there is an eerily silent procession to the sound of mournful drumming.

May/June
Cruces de Mayo (Crosses of May) Each neighbourhood of the city makes a decorative outdoor cross-cum-altar for itself on this

day. The best ones are to be seen in the Albaicín and Realejo. Although there is a competition to choose the best cross, mostly this fiesta is an occasion to fill the streets with life for a day, to sing songs, and to eat broad beans and drink the local Costa wine.

Corpus Christi

For the week around Corpus Christi the city heads out to a purpose-built fairground. Well-to-do men dress in their best riding gear and saunter up and down on horseback while women in typical Andalucían flamenco dresses ride in carriages or dance *sevillanas*, the typical flamenco-style dances originating from Seville.

PUBLIC HOLIDAYS
Año Nuevo (New Year's Day) 1 Jan
Día de Reyes (Epiphany) 6 Jan
Andalucía Day 28 Feb
Jueves Santo (Maundy Thursday) 5 Apr 2012, 28 Mar 2013, 17 Apr 2014
Viernes Santo (Good Friday) 6 Apr 2012, 29 Mar 2013, 18 Apr 2014
Día del Trabajo (Labour Day) 1 May
Asunción de la Virgen (Day of the Assumption) 15 Aug
Día de la Hispanidad (Spain's National Day) 12 Oct
Todos los Santos (All Saints' Day) 1 Nov
Día de la Constitución (Constitution Day) 6 Dec
La Inmaculada Concepción (Immaculate Conception) 8 Dec
Día de Navidad (Christmas Day) 25 Dec

The legacy of the Moors

You can't move in Granada without being reminded that for 750 years the city was under the dominion of the Moors – the Islamic civilisation of southern Spain more properly known as Al Andalus. Granada was the last bastion of the last Muslim kingdom in Europe, and it is impossible to understand the city, its history, its architecture or its traditions without fully appreciating the lingering impact of this.

Yet Granada hasn't always been proud of its past. In the wake of the Reconquest, mosques were converted into churches as fast as humanly possible; castles and palaces – including the Alhambra – were treated to 'Christian' makeovers; and the rambling, inscrutable oriental street pattern of much of the city centre was straightened out according to Renaissance fashion, leaving only the Albaicín in its original state.

But there was no getting away from the legacy of the Moors. The map of Spain is sprinkled with Arabic place names and the Spanish language would be much poorer without the many words derived from Arabic. Moorish craft traditions still flourish. In the countryside, crops introduced by the Moors are still grown, watered by the same ingenious irrigation systems in use 600 or more years ago.

Today, all things Moorish are back in fashion and every last lingering trace of Al Andalus is treated as a source of pride. The Alhambra might be the most stunning reminder of the civilisation that once was, but you can explore the vanished world of Muslim Spain throughout Andalucía by following a series of routes laid out by an organisation based in Granada's Corral del Carbón, the

Legado Andalusi (Legacy of Al Andalus ⓐ Plaza Isabel la Católica 1–5 ⓣ (958) 225 995 ⓦ www.legadoandalusi.es). Leaflets explaining each route are available (free) from Granada's tourist offices.

⬤ *Exquisite Moorish artistry is best seen at the Alhambra*

History

There was probably a prehistoric settlement on the site of modern Granada before the Romans built the town of Iliberis in the 1st century AD. In the 5th century, on the break-up of the Roman Empire, it came under Visigothic rule.

When, in 711, armies from North Africa overran the Iberian peninsula, Granada, then known as Elvira, soon fell into their hands. But it was still a place of little significance, overshadowed by neighbouring Córdoba, the capital of the caliphate which ruled over Muslim Spain or Al Andalus.

Internal divisions led to the fall of the caliphate in the 11th century, and it broke up into small kingdoms. One of these grew up with the city of Granada as its hub. By now the kings of northern Spain had begun the Reconquest of the south in the name of Christianity, but Granada was destined to be the last bit of territory to defy them.

Muhammad ibn Nasr, the first of the Nasrid dynasty, expanded the borders of Granada to stretch across southern Spain from the Atlantic coast to Almería. Under his rule work began on the magnificent fortress-palace of the Alhambra, the finest achievement of art and architecture produced by the Islamic civilisation of Spain.

Cut off from the rest of the Muslim world, the kingdom of Granada survived until the 15th century when King Fernando of Aragon and Queen Isabel of Castile, the so-called Reyes Católicos (Catholic Monarchs), decided to force its rendition. The fall of Granada on 2 January 1492 brought the unification of Spain, but it was also the start of a long period of decline for the city as attention shifted to Seville and the newly founded capital of Madrid.

Only in the 19th century was Granada 'rediscovered' by foreign travellers, particularly the American writer Washington Irving (see page 62). The Alhambra, which until this time had been wilfully neglected as the embarrassing reminder of heathen times, was at last treated as part of the national heritage.

But Spain was living through turbulent times as regimes came and went. The Spanish Civil War broke out in July 1936 and the city was taken by the rebels under General Franco. Spain emerged from the war in 1939 and endured dictatorship until Franco's death in 1975.

The ensuing transition to democracy brought decentralisation and modernisation, and Granada is now the capital city of one of the eight provinces that make up the region of Andalucía.

🔺 *Plaque displaying the Catholic Monarchs and Christopher Columbus*

Lifestyle

Southern Spain lives at a different pace to much of the rest of Europe and you'd be wise to fit in with it. The day in Granada begins slowly and the morning is long. Lunchtime is late by the standards of most visitors: only tourist-oriented restaurants start serving before 14.00 and it is not unusual to sit down to a full meal after 15.00. A long digestive break follows with or without a siesta, according to personal preference and the time of year. In the summer it makes sense to take a nap in the heat of the day so as to be refreshed and ready to go out when the temperature gets bearable again in the evening. The afternoon only begins at 16.00–17.00 and many people still have half a working day ahead of them before clocking off at 21.00 or so. Dinner is at 22.00 or even 23.00 but is not as heavy as lunch. The long gaps between meals are often filled with mini-meals in a bar or café: a late breakfast at around 11.00; *merienda* (something generally sweet) at 18.00 or 19.00; and tapas at any time the fancy takes.

Granadinos in general – there are exceptions – pride themselves on having a more relaxed attitude to time than people in larger cities. They leave room in life for spontaneity and the unplanned, often at the expense of punctuality. If two friends arrange to meet in a bar, for example, neither will be surprised if the other is an hour or so late, having met up with other friends on the way and stopped to have a drink with them out of courtesy.

Less attractively, Granadinos have a reputation for being brusque, at times to the point of rudeness, but most people you will meet will be only too pleased to help you find your way or buy what you want in a shop.

Particularly important in this gregarious country is to show respect for other people. Always say hello when you enter a shop, bar or any other public place: *buenos días* during the day and *buenas tardes* (good afternoon/evening) from about 19.00 or 20.00 on, and *adiós* when you leave.

⬤ *Pavement café in the Plaza Nueva*

Culture

Some locals grumble that Granada is a parochial backwater when it comes to the arts, but it is unfair to compare it with larger cities such as Madrid and Barcelona, or even Seville, and if you arrive without preconceptions you'll probably be agreeably surprised. The city has many good exhibition spaces – several of which are in historic buildings – and its music, theatre and dance venues receive their share of international acts on tour.

Granada's two most famous creator-sons are the classical composer Manuel de Falla (1876–1946) and his friend the poet Federico García Lorca, whose early and violent death in 1936 (see page 20) has only enhanced his reputation. Falla wasn't born in Granada, but he lived here from 1921 to 1939 and the city's main concert hall is named after him. Two of his best-loved pieces are *Nights in the Gardens of Spain* and *The Three-Cornered Hat*.

Lorca was a great admirer of gypsy culture and he'd be delighted to know that contemporary and traditional flamenco music and dance (not to be confused with the shows for tourists, see page 100) are now being taken seriously by audiences and critics. Genuine performances can be experienced throughout the city, particularly in the Sacromonte area (see page 96).

There's plenty of home-grown contemporary art too, this being the kind of place that inspires creative types. And look out especially for exhibitions of the art (and science) of an earlier era, Muslim Spain – an area in which Granada inevitably beats other cities hands down.

Federico García Lorca by Ciriaco Párraga

THE MURDER OF LORCA

At dawn on 19 August 1936, during the early days of the Civil War, one of Spain's greatest poets and playwrights was abducted from a friend's house in Granada and shot by right-wing militiamen in circumstances that have never been fully explained. Federico García Lorca came from a good family and, although he had left-wing leanings, he was not overtly political. He was, however, libertarian and a homosexual – just the sort of person who wouldn't fit into the authoritarian, ultra-Catholic country that Franco and his cronies were planning to turn Spain into. Granada had fallen into the rebel military's hands at the start of the war and it was probably only a matter of time before Lorca was rounded up as an example to other nonconformists.

Still, in his 37 years of life, Lorca made a reputation for himself, which has endured and made him a secular, literary saint today. He was heavily influenced by the gypsy culture of Andalucía and a champion of the socially disenfranchised, and of women. His best-known plays include *Blood Wedding*, *Yerma* and *The House of Bernarda Alba*.

His birthplace in the town of Fuente Vaqueros (15 km/ 9 miles northwest of Granada) can be visited, as can his house in Granada, the Huerta de San Vicente (see page 78), which has been turned into a museum.

▶ *Flamenco dresses for sale*

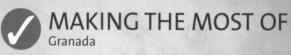

MAKING THE MOST OF
Granada

Shopping

The main shopping district of Granada is a rectangle formed by the Gran Vía de Colón, Calle Reyes Católicos, Calle Alhóndiga and Plaza Trinidad, but you can continue shopping down Calle de Recogidas and in the streets between Puerta Real and El Realejo. The narrow streets and squares here are either pedestrianised or almost traffic-free, making it easy to move about, although there are often crowds of shoppers and bar-hoppers to contend with.

Some shops – particularly in the Alcaicería (in the centre, see page 82) and on the Cuesta de Gomérez leading up to the Alhambra – cater exclusively for tourists and it's rare to find authentic craft goods in such places. If you want a high-quality souvenir from Granada, you should choose a serious, specialised craft shop and be prepared to pay for good workmanship.

Like everywhere else in Europe, it seems, there is a trend towards out-of-town shopping in vast complexes of brand outlets grouped around a hypermarket. You might find a loss-leading bargain in such places but you are unlikely to find anything

WHAT TO BUY

Pottery is Granada's trademark craft. Guitars are also made in the city. Another good idea for a souvenir is something edible from a delicatessen, such as a bottle of extra virgin olive oil or some ham cured in the mountain air of Trevélez (see page 119).

authentically local for sale. Far better is to favour the many
small, independent shops that the centre of Granada is still blessed
with. Prices are not always higher than in shopping centres –
that is a myth – but it is difficult to browse undisturbed and you
will be forced to practise your Spanish to get what you want.

Spain's own department store chain, **El Corte Inglés**
(ⓦ www.elcorteingles.es), is a one-stop shopper's paradise.
A temple to the joys of retail commerce, it's a place in which to

⬧ *Look out for small, specialised craft shops*

USEFUL SHOPPING PHRASES

What time do the shops open/close?
¿A qué hora abren/cierran las tiendas?
¿A kay ora abren/theeyerran las teeyendas?

How much is this?
¿Cuánto es?
¿Cwantoe es?

Can I try this on?
¿Puedo probarme esto?
¿Pwedo probarme esto?

My size is ...
Mi número es el ...
Mee noomero es el ...

I'll take this one.
Me llevo éste.
Meh yievo esteh.

This is too large/too small/too expensive.
Do you have any others?
Es muy grande/muy pequeño/muy caro. ¿Tienen más?
Es mooy grandeh/mooy pekenio/mooy karo. ¿Teeyenen mas?

waft around and browse before you give your credit card a trot out. You'll find almost anything you are looking for here, including fashion, books and newspapers in English, maps and CDs of Spanish music. The in-store supermarket is a cut above the average, as is shown by its range of exquisite gourmet foods. There are branches at Carrera del Genil 20–22 (☎ (958) 223 240) and at Calle Arabial 95 and 97 (☎ (958) 217 600), the latter specialising in home ware.

Eating & drinking

Installing yourself in a succession of bars, cafés and restaurants is one of the delights of a visit to Granada. The city has a wide choice of places to eat and drink from the old-fashioned and quaint to the vibrantly modern.

For the most part the cuisine is 'typically Andalucían', which means straightforward meat, fish, seafood and vegetable dishes prepared and served with the minimum of complication and formality. With such an abundance of good fresh ingredients to hand there's no need to disguise them with rich sauces. As this is southern Spain, most dishes have olive oil lurking in them somewhere and dairy foods are used minimally. Bear in mind that vegetables and salads are generally served separately as a starter and will not be included with the main dish, which is usually meat or fish served alone or with chips.

The main meal in Spain is in the middle of the day, and most restaurants offer a cheaper menu, *menu del día*, which typically consists of three courses with a bottle of the house wine included. This is certainly the best way to fill up without spending a lot.

PRICE CATEGORIES

Average price for a three-course meal (*menu del día* if there is one) for one person, excluding drinks, but including tax:
£ up to €20   ££ €20–40   £££ over €40
Ratings for cafés and bars are:
£ inexpensive   ££ moderately priced   £££ expensive

When looking for a restaurant the best advice is to eat where the locals eat and avoid anywhere that displays photographs of its dishes outside. If in doubt, follow a group of hungry students, who will know where to make their money go furthest.

Spain's main failing is its dessert menu, which all too often reduces to a piece of fresh fruit, a scoop of ice cream or the

◔ Dishes of the day

ubiquitous *flan* – crème caramel. But it makes up for this deficiency by being strong on sweet snacks. Granada has several excellent cake shops, *pastelerías*, offering a choice of something to go with a coffee or to fill the long gap between lunch and dinner.

A popular breakfast or midnight snack during fiestas is a portion of *churros* – deep-fried sticks of batter that are best enjoyed dunked into a cup of deliciously thick hot chocolate.

Where Granada excels is in its tapas bars. Even the most sophisticated restaurants are likely to have a bar attached where you can eat well without having to order a full meal or eat formally. By tradition, a tapa is served free with each drink in Granada – it will arrive in front of you after a couple of minutes' delay. Most bars serve tapas in a set order so you get something different with each round of drinks. What you get is a matter of luck or knowing the bar. A tapa can be as simple as a saucer of olives or crisps; or it might be a slice of *jamón serrano* or wedge of cured sheep's cheese, but it might just as well be something more substantial such as a selection of fried fish, a seafood salad or a portion of paella.

If you want a larger portion, ask for a *ración*. But take care: tapas and *raciones* can easily add up to more than a full menu in a restaurant.

The big thing about tapas is that they are available any time of day or night: you'll rarely hear anyone in Granada tell you the kitchen is closed and there's nothing to eat.

Incidentally, tapas are often a godsend to vegetarians visiting Spain. If nothing else, almost every bar can offer up a *ración* of meat-free salad, a slice of the old standby *tortilla de patata* (potato omelette) or wedges of cheese.

USEFUL DINING PHRASES

I would like a table for ... people.
Quisiera una mesa para ... personas.
Keyseeyera oona mesa para ... personas.

May I have the bill, please?
¿Podría traerme la cuenta, por favor?
¿Pordreea trayerme la cwenta, por fabor?

Waiter/Waitress!
¡Camarero/Camarera!
¡Camareroe/Camarera!

Could I have it well cooked/medium/rare, please?
Por favor, ¿la carne bien pasada/al punto/poco hecha?
Por favor, ¿la kahrrne beeyen passada/al poontoh/poco etcha?

I am a vegetarian. Does this contain meat?
Soy vegetariano/a. ¿Tiene carne este plato?
Soy begetahreeahnoh/ah. ¿Teeyene carneh esteh plahtoh?

Where is the toilet, please?
¿Dónde están los servicios, por favor?
¿Donde estan los serbeetheeos, por fabor?

I would like a cup of/two cups of/another coffee/tea.
Quisiera una taza de/dos tazas de/otra taza de café/té.
Keyseeyera oona tatha dey/dos tathas dey/otra tatha dey kafey/tey.

Entertainment & nightlife

Granada offers a generous choice of entertainment from low- to highbrow, depending on your taste. Largely because of the climate, but also because of the pattern of the working day, nights out begin late and go on later, especially in summer, when daytime temperatures are too hot to do anything except relax indoors. During fiestas (see page 8) there will be enough going on in the streets and you won't need to look for amusements elsewhere. The most popular entertainment for foreign visitors to the city is flamenco music and dance (see page 96).

For details of what's on in Granada during your stay, ask at the local tourist office, where you'll be able to pick up a free guide to events. Or see the following websites:

ⓦ www.pocketguia.es (in Spanish only)

ⓦ www.guiadelocio.com/granada

Two online agencies specialising in booking tickets for entertainment in Spain are:

ⓦ www.entradas.com ① (902) 221 622

ⓦ www.servicaixa.com ① (902) 332 211

Most foreign films screened in Spain are dubbed into Spanish. Few original-version (VO – for *versión original*) English and American films are shown in Granada and your best bet to see one is at the university's film club **Cineclub Universitario** (ⓔ Facultad de Ciencias ① (958) 243 484 ⓦ www.ugr.es) or language school **Centro de Lenguas Modernas** (ⓐ Placeta del Hospicio Viejo ① (958) 215 660 ⓦ www.ugr.es).

● *Head to Sacromonte for lively flamenco shows*

Granada's main theatre is **Teatro Isabel la Católica** (🅰 Acera del Casino ☎ (958) 222 907), and performances are all in Spanish. Perhaps more interesting to the visitor is the **Centro Cultural Manuel de Falla** (🅰 Calle Antequeruela Alta 11 ☎ (958) 222 907 🌐 www.manueldefalla.org), which puts on a programme of classical music and dance by visiting companies.

There are two shifts of nightlife in Granada. If you prefer an early bed, you can happily do the rounds of tapas bars until 23.00 or so. It's only then that serious night people go out to start their evening in a *bar de copas* – a bar made for drinking (shorts mainly), with few or no chairs and low light levels. Most such bars pride themselves on the attractiveness of their counter staff and their select taste in music. A few have DJs and dance floors or put on live acts, and some charge admission accordingly. Only after 24.00 do people move on to clubs (*discotecas*), which may stay open until 06.00 or later. Nightlife areas shift with the times, but the Carrera del Darro and Campo del Príncipe are good places to start out.

ARTS FESTIVALS
Festival Internacional de Tango (International Tango Festival) (early March) This festival, now over two decades old, remains popular. ☎ (958) 291 796 🌐 www.eltango.com

Festival Internacional de Música y Danza (International Festival of Music and Dance) (last two weeks of June and the first week of July) Over 50 years old and still going strong, this festival uses the Alhambra and Generalife among its venues. ☎ (958) 221 844 🌐 www.granadafestival.org

Encuentros Flamencos (Festival de Otoño: Autumn Festival)
(October) An annual celebration of flamenco that takes place
in Peña Flamenca La Platería (see page 100). ❶ (958) 229 344
Ⓦ www.granada.org

Festival de Jazz de Granada (Granada Jazz Festival) (November)
A jazz festival that attracts top names. ❷ Casa Morisca, Calle
Horno del Oro 14 ❶ (958) 215 980 Ⓦ www.jazzgranada.es

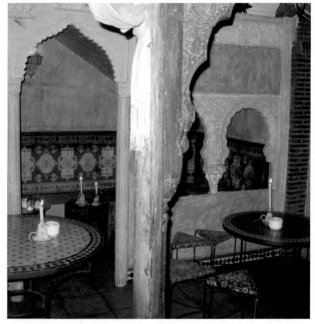

🔺 A tetería *(tea shop)* is an atmospheric place for a drink or two

Sport & relaxation

Granada has good sports facilities for a city of its size and it's also extremely well located for outdoor activities. In the winter you can head for the mountains to go skiing, and in summer descend on the beaches of the Costa Tropical for a variety of watersports. If you are more in the mood to relax, on the other hand, where better than an Arab bathhouse (the equivalent of Turkish baths)?

SPECTATOR SPORTS
Bullfighting

It is easy to condemn bullfighting as ritualised animal cruelty, but it's worth taking a moment to try to understand its hold on the Spanish psyche, particularly in Andalucía. Although bullfighting was banned in Catalunya in mid-2010, it remains popular here and is treated in much of the local media as something between a sport and an art. If you want to attend a bullfight, head for **Granada's bullring** (ⓐ Avenida del Doctor Olóriz 14 ❶ (958) 200 727), 1.5 km (1 mile) northwest of the city centre. The season runs from April to October.

PARTICIPATION SPORTS
Skiing

The Sierra Nevada ski resort enjoys a season that lasts until the first week of May (aided by snow cannons) with almost guaranteed sunshine and blue skies all the while. Regular skiers say it offers the best spring snow conditions in Europe. The ski station is 32 km (20 miles) by road from Granada at an altitude of 2,100 m (6,890 ft). Its top station is at 3,300 m (10,827 ft), just 100 m (330 ft) below the summit of La Veleta, Spain's third-highest peak. Altogether there are 23 lifts serving 80 pistes totalling 84 km (52 miles). The longest run, the Pista del Águila, descends for almost 6 km (4 miles). There is also a snowboard park and a cross-country skiing circuit. On Saturday evening some of the runs are open for night-skiing. As well as hotels and restaurants the ski station has two crèches.

RELAXATION

Arab baths

Aljibe de San Miguel (ⓐ Calle de San Miguel Alta 41 ⓣ (958) 522 867 ⓦ www.aljibesanmiguel.es) is a fully equipped Arab-style bathhouse that offers various additional therapies and massages.

Hammam Baños Arabes (ⓐ Calle Santa Ana 16 ⓣ (958) 229 978 ⓦ www.granada.hammamspain.com) is a re-creation of an Arab bathhouse decorated with tiled mosaics and including a *teteria*.

🔺 *Pedalos at the ready on Salobreña beach, Costa Tropical*

Accommodation

Granada has a good choice of places to stay, some reasonably inexpensive. Hotels are officially ranked from one to five stars, but this doesn't tell you much except the quantity of facilities; atmosphere and the standard of service do not always correspond to stars, and neither do prices. Generally cheaper are *hostales* (not to be confused with youth hostels) and *pensiones*. These are guesthouses that are likely to have en-suite rooms but not 24-hour reception or room service, and they may not offer any meals apart from breakfast. A well-cared-for, family-run *pensión* or *hostal* can be a more friendly place to stay, however, than a large, modern hotel armed with all creature comforts, and they represent better value. Better hotels, *hostales* and *pensiones* have heating in winter and air conditioning in summer.

A few hotels are located on the same hill as the Alhambra, which makes them convenient for visiting the city's main monument, but they are not so handy for the city centre below. The Albaicín has some charming small places to stay, but many of them are on steep and narrow streets where buses, cars and taxis do not reach, and you might have to walk to get to them.

PRICE CATEGORIES

The price symbols indicate the approximate price of an en-suite room for two people for one night in high season, including tax:

£ up to €60 **££** €60–120 **£££** over €120

City-centre hotels are mainly modern and functional; their location offers a strategic base from which it is easy to get to the rest of the city, but note that some streets may be noisy day and night.

If you want guaranteed peace and quiet, there are several hotels in Granada's rural hinterland, but you'll have to be prepared to commute in for sightseeing.

HOTELS

Fonda Sánchez £ Two minutes' walk from the Gran Vía and almost as close to the cathedral, this small hotel has simple, well-lit rooms at a very good price for such a central location. ⓐ Plaza de la Universidad 1, 2ª (The city centre) ⓣ (958) 278 235 ⓦ www.fondasanchez.com

Hostal Camino Real £ Located on the new access road to the Alhambra, this *hostal* run by an English-speaking family is also convenient for the Sierra Nevada. One of the ten rooms is equipped for disabled travellers. ⓐ Avenida Santa María de la Alhambra 2–1A (main entrance on Calle Radua) (The Alhambra) ⓣ (958) 210 057 ⓦ www.hostalcaminoreal.com

Hotel Santa Isabel la Real ££ A pretty boutique hotel in a historic building at the top of the Albaicín. It has distant views of the Alhambra from the top of its patio. ⓐ Calle de Santa Isabel la Real 19 (The Albaicín & Sacromonte) ⓣ (958) 294 658 ⓦ www.hotel santaisabellareal.com

Hotel Los Tilos ££ This attractive traditional hotel overlooks a lovely square that hosts a daily flower market. Rooms have been recently renovated and are spacious and comfortable. There is a small rooftop terrace for catching the rays. ⓐ Plaza Bib-Rambla (The city centre) ⓣ (958) 266 712 ⓦ www.hotellostilos.com

Hotel Zaguán del Darro ££ Pleasant hotel in a 16th-century building in which most rooms have views of the Alhambra or River Darro. There is a bar-cum-restaurant on the ground floor. ⓐ Carrera del Darro 23 (The Albaicín & Sacromonte) ⓣ (958) 215 730 ⓦ www.hotelzaguan.com

⬤ *The attractive lobby at the Zaguán hotel*

Palacio de Santa Inés ££ A charming hotel in a restored old mansion at the bottom of the Albaicín. The patio is decorated with murals thought to be by a disciple of Raphael. Some of the rooms have views of the Alhambra. ⓐ Cuesta de Santa Inés 9 (The Albaicín & Sacromonte) ⓣ (958) 222 362 ⓦ www. palaciosantaines.com

Parador San Francisco £££ One of the jewels in the state-run chain of Parador hotels, this one has an incomparable setting beside the Alhambra and for this reason it is both expensive and usually fully booked. Reserve well ahead to ensure a room. ⓐ Calle Real de la Alhambra (The Alhambra) ⓣ (958) 221 440 ⓦ www.parador.es

SELF-CATERING (SHORT LETS)

Cuevas El Abanico £ A suite of self-contained one- or two-bedroom caves with tiled floors and whitewashed walls, each with its own kitchen and some with terraces. Like all caves, these enjoy a constant temperature: cool in summer; warm in winter. The minimum stay is two days. ⓐ Verea de Enmedio 89 (The Albaicín & Sacromonte) ⓣ (958) 226 199 ⓦ www.el-abanico.com

El Numero 8 £ An Albaicín house that has been divided into delightful self-contained apartments for the independent traveller. There is Wi-Fi and a shared roof terrace from which there are views of the Alhambra. ⓐ La Casa de Rafa (near Aljibe de las Tomasas – call from the square to be escorted to the house) (The Albaicín & Sacromonte) ⓣ (958) 220 682 ⓦ www.elnumero8.com

YOUTH HOSTELS

Oasis Backpackers Hostel £ A very cheap place to stay but nevertheless with good facilities if you are happy to crash in a dormitory (with en-suite bathroom). Sheets, breakfast, Internet access, tea and coffee and the use of a personal safe are all included in the price. **ⓐ** Placeta Correo Viejo 3 (in the lower part of the Albaicín just above Calle Elvira) (The Albaicín & Sacromonte) **ⓣ** (958) 215 848 **ⓦ** www.oasisgranada.com

CAMPSITES

Camping María Eugenia The closest campsite to the city, about 3 km (2 miles) from the centre. Open year-round. **ⓐ** Avenida de Andalucía 190 (A329 from Granada towards Málaga) **ⓣ** (958) 200 606 **ⓦ** www.vayacamping.net/mariaeugenia

🔺 *Interesting murals at the Palacio de Santa Inés*

THE BEST OF GRANADA

Whether you have days of leisure to spare or a few hours to cram everything essential into, these are some of the sights and activities you'll probably want to fit into your stay.

TOP 10 ATTRACTIONS

- **Albaicín** This labyrinthine former Muslim quarter on the hill opposite the Alhambra is a place to explore on foot, taking your time (see page 86).

- **Alhambra** The incomparable fortress-palace, exquisitely decorated within, is Granada's must-see monument (see page 58).

- **The Alpujarras** An area of deep valleys with long green slopes on the other side of the Sierra Nevada from the city. Scenic walking country and cute villages (see page 115).

- **Capilla Real** The two monarchs who unified Spain lie under magnificent sepulchres in this royal chapel next to the cathedral (see page 71).

- **Corral del Carbón** A former caravanserai (roadside inn). Small and discreet but redolent of times gone by (see page 77).

- **Flamenco** The emblematic music and dance of southern Spain comes in many forms but is always performed with passion (see page 96).

- **Generalife** The gardens of this palace connected to the Alhambra (although they can be visited separately) are among the best in Spain (see page 67).

- **Sacromonte** Many people live in caves in Granada's traditional gypsy quarter that winds along a pretty valley (see page 92).

- **Skiing** Europe's southernmost ski resort – and Spain's highest – is close to the city. It offers excellent spring snow conditions and guaranteed sunshine (see page 33).

- **Tapas bars** The city has endless bars in all sizes and styles all serving tapas – tasty snacks – usually free with each drink you order (see page 27).

🔻 *Moorish tiles in the Palacio de Comares, Alhambra*

Suggested itineraries

HALF-DAY: GRANADA IN A HURRY

With just a morning or an afternoon, the only way to spend it is in the Alhambra, and even then you won't see it all so concentrate on the Royal Palaces. Make sure you have reserved your ticket before arriving.

1 DAY: TIME TO SEE A LITTLE MORE

You might want to rush around the Alhambra in the morning or afternoon, but you'd be better off devoting most of the day to getting there, around it and back. A stroll in the less hectic Albaicín quarter would make a good contrast and you'll certainly want to fit in a few tapas bars at midday and/or in the evening.

○ Don't miss the stunning Generalife gardens and palace

THE SIGN OF THE POMEGRANATE

Everywhere you go in Granada you'll see the same symbol repeated over and over again, appearing everywhere from bank logos to manhole covers: a pomegranate fruit so ripe that it splits open to reveal the succulent pips within. Although the word for pomegranate in Spanish is *granada*, this is only a coincidence as the name of the city has a different derivation. The conquerors of the Moorish kingdom incorporated the pomegranate into their own coat of arms as part of the spoils of victory (and from there it found its way on to Spain's national coat of arms).

2–3 DAYS: TIME TO SEE MUCH MORE

Allow the better part of one day to see the Alhambra and Generalife properly and build your visit around that. If you can, go up to the Albaicín first and admire the view of the Alhambra from it. You'll also want to spend a few hours in the city centre, visiting the Capilla Real and the Corral del Carbón and doing some shopping. Two nights will give you time to hop around several tapas bars and even find a favourite one.

LONGER: ENJOYING GRANADA TO THE FULL

With a week or more you'll have time to fit in everything you want to see and do. If this is your first visit to southern Spain, you'll probably want to get out of the city altogether and perhaps go down to the coast for one day and to Córdoba to see its famous mosque, which makes the ideal complement to the Alhambra.

Something for nothing

To see the best of Granada you don't need to spend much money and with a little imagination you can have a great time on a shoestring budget. It is a great city just to walk around – the atmosphere and the views of the Alhambra are free. It's not difficult to devise a two- or three-day itinerary for strolling around streets and squares with frequent stops to watch street life go by from different angles. You can easily spend a day alone meandering around the delightful streets of the Albaicín, wondering at the view from the Mirador de San Nicolás, and continuing to Sacromonte, stopping in some shady little square on the way. Turning pennilessness into a virtue, you can concentrate your time on seeking out the less common sights – old Arab gateways, walls, cisterns and the like – that other visitors don't bother to go and look for.

True, you won't see the inside of the Alhambra if you can't afford the price of the entrance ticket, but you can still amble around the parts which are open to everyone, and if you are an EU citizen you can visit the Alhambra's museum in the Palacio de Carlos V for free. You can also visit the Museo Arqueológico y Etnológico (Archaeological Museum), the sumptuous Iglesia de San Juan de Dios and the old bathhouse of El Bañuelo for free.

Other sights that are free to get into are the Corral del Carbón, the Casa Museo Max Moreau (the house of a Belgian artist in the Albaicín), the Palacio de Dar Al-Horra (also in the Albaicín), the Museo de Artes y Costumbres Populares (a folk museum) in the Casa de los Tiros, and the Centro de Arte Contemporáneo José Guerrero (a gallery of contemporary art).

As a bonus, if you happen to be in Granada during a fiesta – especially Holy Week or the Corpus Christi fair – you have all the free outdoor entertainment you could ask for.

◆ *Head up to the Alhambra for fantastic views*

When it rains

You're unlikely to get rain on a summer visit to Granada, but you may well get a shower or a downpour if you are here between autumn and spring. While the city is certainly not at its best under overcast skies, and with rain drizzling down the back of your neck, there are ways to modify your itinerary in response to the weather. You won't be much interested in squares in the Albaicín or restaurant terraces with views of the Alhambra, but there are other things to do and see. If you have reserved tickets for the Alhambra, you won't be able to change your plans at the last minute and unfortunately you won't see the place looking its best. Parts of the monument are, however, under cover – you'll just have to put off the Generalife gardens until another time.

The main change to your visit will be that you will have to get around by bus and hop between shelters. The city doesn't have any large museums in which to lose yourself for long periods, but you could pass an hour in the Museo Arqueológico y Etnológico and another in the folk museum in the Casa de los Tiros. The Capilla Real and cathedral are other dry sights in the centre. Another, leisurely, way to avoid the weather is to go to an Arab bathhouse (see page 34).

In the city centre you can hop between shops across the narrow streets, but a safer bet is to go to the department store of El Corte Inglés, where you can while away a few hours.

Another option is to buy a copy of *Tales of the Alhambra* (see page 62) and sit reading it in a café. If you can last until evening falls, you'll then be able to link up a series of tapas bars and places with live music and barely notice the weather as you drift between them.

⬤ *Spend a rainy hour or two at the Museo Arqueológico y Etnológico*

On arrival

Granada is easy to get into and out of. Take an hour or so to familiarise yourself with the street layout and the main minibus routes.

TIME DIFFERENCE
Spain follows Central European Time (CET). From late March to late October the clocks are put forward by one hour.

ARRIVING
By air
Granada's airport is **Federico García Lorca** (international code: GRX Ⓦ www.aena.es), 17 km (11 miles) from the city on the A92 motorway towards Antequera and Málaga. There is a bus from the airport's arrivals area to the Gran Vía de Colón in the centre of Granada. The bus journey takes around 35 minutes and stops at the Palacio de Congresos (next to Bar Ventorillo), Acera del Darro, Jardines del Triunfo, the train station, the bus station and Avenida de Andalucía. As running times vary, it is advisable to check with the operating company, **J. González 9** (❶ (958) 490 164 Ⓦ www.autocaresjosegonzalez.com), to avoid a long wait. The only alternative is a **taxi** (❶ (958) 245 200).

There is a much larger choice of flights to **Málaga airport** (❶ (952) 048 484 Ⓦ www.aena.es), which is 130 km (81 miles) away. There are buses from Málaga bus station to Granada approximately every hour during the day, and the journey takes about two hours.

By rail

Granada's **railway station** (ⓐ Avenida Andaluces ⓝ Bus: 4, 6 or 11) is off Avenida de la Constitución, about 1.5 km (1 mile) west of the city centre. Check the RENFE website (ⓦ www.renfe.es) for comprehensive timetables and prices. There are twice-daily trains to Madrid, Valencia and Barcelona, as well as numerous services to other local and national towns and cities.

Granada is a stop on the route of the private luxury train the **Al Andalus Expreso** (ⓣ (902) 169 900 ⓦ www.alandalus-expreso.com).

By road

The **coach station** (ⓐ Carretera de Jaén ⓣ (902) 422 242 ⓦ www.alsa.es ⓝ Bus: 3 or 33) is 2.5 km (1½ miles) northwest of the centre past the bullring. The largest coach operator is **Alsina Graells** (ⓣ (958) 185 480 ⓦ www.alsa.es), with daily services to Seville, Madrid, Córdoba and the Alpujarras.

⬤ *A Credibus card is useful if you need to make several journeys*

Granada

0   150 metres

0   150 yards

SACROMONTE

Abadía del Sacromonte

CAMINO DEL SACROMONTE

Iglesia del Salvador

Mirador de San Nicolás

ALBAICÍN

CARRIL DE SAN AGUSTÍN

CUESTA DEL CHAPIZ

GUINEA CAÑELLOS S. AGUSTÍN

CL VICTORIA

CANDIL

SANTIAGO

GLORIA

IN DE LOS REYES

ZAFRA

Río Darro

PASEO DE PADRE MANJÓN

Generalife

CAMINO DE LA SILLA

CARRERA DEL DARRO

CTA DEL REY CHICO

Convento de Sta Catalina de Zafra

Museo Arqueológico y Etnológico

Puente de Cadí

Palacios Nazaríes

Alcazaba

Palacio de Carlos V

ALHAMBRA

Parador de Turismo

Entrance to Generalife

DE GOMÉREZ

BOSQUE DE LA ALHAMBRA

Puerta de las Granadas

Ticket Office

CALLEJÓN NIÑO DEL ROLLO

PLAZA ARQUITECTO GARCÍA

Fundación Rodríguez-Acosta

CTA STA CATALINA

ALAMILLOS

PEÑA PARTIDA DE PAREDES

PLECADERO ALTO

CTA DEL REALEJO

EL REALEJO

ANTEQUERUELA BAJA

Museo de Artes Costumbres opulares

PC DEL REALEJO

COCHERAS

CIÓN DE VARGAS

CAMINO NUEVO DEL CEMENTERIO

PLAZA CAMPO DEL PRINCIPE

CUARTELILLO

BELÉN

CTA STO DOMINGO

CALLE DE SANTIAGO

ACO P CO DE LUCENA

CON CALLE DEL SEÑOR

CUESTA DEL CALDERO

AIXA C REAL STO DOMINGO

CALLE DE SOLARES

CALLE DE MOLINOS

SAN MATÍAS

VISTILLA DE LOS ÁNGELES

CTA DE ESCORIAZA

LAS MOLINOS

PASEO DE LAS PALMAS

PASEO DEL SALÓN

PASEO DE LA BOMBA

PASEO DEL SALÓN

PASEO DE LA BOMBA

Río Genil

...POI

✝ .....Cathedral

ℹ .....Information

⊘ ...Police Station

✈ .....Airport

🚉 .....Railway Stn

🚌 .....Bus Station

✚ .....Hospital

If you have to drive into Granada, it's best to have a secure parking place lined up and head straight for it. Avoid rush hours and driving in the narrow streets of the Albaicín or the city centre. If there is a quieter time to enter or leave the city by car, it is during the lunch break, around 14.00–16.00.

FINDING YOUR FEET

Granada is a lively, busy city and inevitably it has its criminals on the lookout for easy prey. That said, you should have no problems if you always keep your bag and camera close to you and don't stop in a dark alley to look at your map.

ORIENTATION

Granada's main streets are the Gran Vía de Colón and the Calle Reyes Católicos, which meet at the Plaza Isabel la Católica. To the north of here is Plaza Nueva, from where you can get to the Alhambra on foot or by minibus. To the south is another important crossroads, Puerta Real, on which stands the central post office – a useful landmark.

GETTING AROUND

The best way to get from sight to sight is to walk, but to reach the Alhambra, Sacromonte, the upper parts of the Albaicín or outlying sights, you may want to take a bus or taxi.

Bus

You probably won't need to take many buses – see the 'Líneas Turísticas' on page 54 for useful routes. Pay the driver on boarding. If you are going to use buses a lot, buy a

GRANADA CITY PASS (BONO TURÍSTICO)

This swipe card, valid for five days from the date of issue, allows you one free visit each to the Alhambra (you must state the time you want to visit the Nasrid Palaces – see page 65), Generalife, cathedral, Capilla Real (Royal Chapel), Monasterio de San Jerónimo and the Parque de las Ciencias (Science Museum). It also entitles you to ten bus trips and one ticket for the sightseeing bus, City Sightseeing. The price of the card represents a saving of about 30 per cent if you visit all the sights covered. You can buy the pass in Plaza Nueva (at the red kiosk where the Albaicín bus stops), at the Caja Granada bank on Plaza Isabel La Católica 6, or by calling the Bono Turístico information number on ❶ (902) 10 00 95 (English is spoken)

Credibus swipe card from the driver. This covers nine journeys (allowing you 45 minutes to change buses if necessary) and can be topped up as often as needed. For information call ❶ (900) 710 900 ⓦ www.granadadirect.com/transporte/bonobus-granada

Tour bus

City Sightseeing (❶ (902) 101 081 ⓦ www.city-sightseeing.com) offers a comprehensive hop on–hop off service on an open-topped double decker running around every half-hour. The main stop is outside the cathedral and the 90-minute tour takes in about 40 monuments.

IF YOU GET LOST, TRY ...

Excuse me, do you speak English?
Perdone, ¿habla usted inglés?
Pairdohney, ¿abla oosteth eengless?

Excuse me, is this the right way to the old town/the city centre/the tourist office/the train station/the bus station?
Perdone, ¿por aquí se va al casco antiguo/al centro de la ciudad/a la oficina de turismo/a la estación de trenes/a la estación de autobuses?
Pairdohney, ¿porr akee seh bah al kasko antigwo/al thentroe deh la theeoodath/a la offeetheena deh toorismoe/a la estatheeon dey trenes/a la estatheeon dey awtoebooses?

Taxi

A green light means a taxi is for hire. The fare will be fixed by meter, which may start at a minimum charge.

Servi-Taxi ❶ (958) 400 199
Taxi Genil ❶ (958) 132 323
Teleradio Taxi ❶ (958) 280 654

Car

Narrow streets and traffic jams mean it's not worth trying to drive around the city centre. It is best to explore on foot or by public transport or taxi. For information on car hire see page 129.

❶ *Decorative railings and rooftops*

THE CITY OF
Granada

The Alhambra

No other monument anywhere has quite the allure of the world-famous fortress-palace of the Alhambra, a masterpiece of oriental art and architecture. It's the most popular monument to visit in Spain and it is highly recommended that you book your visit in advance, as a limited number of tickets are sold on the day and they tend to go quickly (see visiting information on page 63).

Rather than one building, the Alhambra is an extraordinary complex of fortifications, palaces, gardens, annexes, bathhouses, prayer halls and sundry other structures dating from both the Muslim era and after.

The Alhambra was built by the Nasrid dynasty of kings, who ruled Granada from the 13th century until the fall of the city. The most stunning part is the suite of royal palaces that mostly date from the 14th century.

They employed the finest architects, artists and craftsmen of their day to create the most extraordinarily elaborate interior decoration, which they probably regarded as being as ephemeral as modern wallpaper.

Working without the aid of modern measuring instruments, they decorated vast surfaces with arabesques in stucco and ingenious mathematical designs of interlocking stars made from pieces of ceramic tiles in vivid colours neatly clipped to precise shapes. The idea of all this, however, was not to overwhelm the viewer but to create harmonious, endlessly repeating patterns that were easy on the eye, thus freeing the mind to think higher thoughts.

Yet, ironically, what is indisputably the highest achievement of Muslim Spain was really a last creative gasp of a people at the end of their stay. While the marvels of the Alhambra were taking shape, Granada was becoming the ever more isolated, last outpost of Islam in Spain. Just over a century after the paint

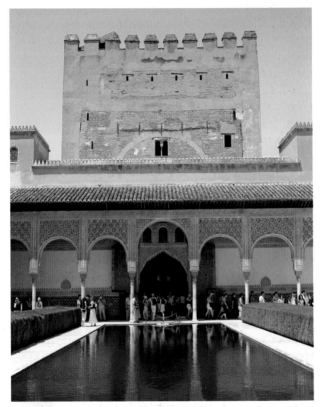

⬧ *The majestic Patio de los Arrayanes, outside the Palacio de Comares*

The Alhambra

0 — 60 metres
0 — 60 yards

Generalife

CAMINO DE LA SILLA

Huertas de la
Alhambra

Jardines Nuevos
del Generalife

RTAL

nes del
artal

MEDINA

Parador de
Turismo

Secano

Entrance to
Generalife

Ticket
Office

POI

61

had dried, the civilisation that inspired such harmony and beauty came to an abrupt end.

After the Reconquest of Granada in 1492, the Alhambra suffered a fluctuating fate. Its new Christian proprietors were loath to admire the beauty of such a heathen place and they didn't know what to do with it.

Only during the 19th century did things begin to look up again for the Alhambra when it attracted the attention of travelling writers and artists who were fascinated by the oriental fantasy of it. In particular, the American writer Washington Irving lived within its walls for a while (see box) and bequeathed to the world a classic book about his experiences.

In 1870 the Alhambra was finally acknowledged to be a unique, valuable and irreplaceable part of Spanish heritage. The subsequent

WASHINGTON IRVING

In 1829 the American writer Washington Irving, who is best remembered for creating the character of Rip Van Winkle, took up residence in the semi-dilapidated and much-neglected Alhambra, which was then occupied by a vestigial garrison of soldiers. Three years later he published his *Tales of the Alhambra* (widely available in the original English in Granada's souvenir shops), which makes fascinating reading before or after visiting the monument itself. It is a blend of travelogue, history and, above all, retelling of tales and myths about the Alhambra and its occupants of old.

work of restoration has sometimes been controversial, and what you see today is often based on scholarly guesswork as much as actual knowledge about the work of architects and artists in 14th-century Moorish Spain.

A good way to approach the Alhambra is to look at it first from the Albaicín (see page 86), then to take a walk (or minibus) up the hill to admire its outer parts and get your bearings. Finally, ticket in hand, plunge yourself into the middle of it. For simplicity, the complex can be divided into four parts: the Alcazaba (or old citadel); the royal palaces (the highlight of the visit); the grounds of the Alhambra, including a street of shops and hotels; and the summer palace of the Generalife, visited chiefly for its gardens. ❶ Note that restoration, maintenance and repair work is being carried out continually and some parts of the monument may be temporarily closed during your visit.

How to visit

A visit to the Alhambra is best planned well in advance. You can turn up on the day and queue for a ticket at the ticket office next to the car park, but unless you are very early tickets may sell out. Far better is to buy your ticket by phone, online or over a bank counter (see page 64) before you arrive in Granada.

If you arrive without a pre-purchased ticket, join the queue for the ticket office or for the automatic ticket machines. These accept either credit cards or cash but charge a €1 commission fee.

The best way to get to the Alhambra is on foot from Plaza Nueva, although it is a long, steep walk up the Cuesta de Gomérez and through the 16th-century Puerta de las Granadas (which is named after the pomegranates that adorn it). A minibus travels the same route from Plaza Nueva. By car, you have to approach the Alhambra along an access road from the southeast, which avoids the city centre. The ticket office is next to the car park (☎ (902) 441 221 🌐 www.alhambra-patronato.es or www.alhambra.org 🕐 08.30–20.00 daily (summer); 08.30–18.00 daily (winter)). You can book your tickets up to three months in advance at 🌐 www.alhambra-tickets.es. You can also buy your tickets direct from La Caixa bank ATMs. If you haven't booked in advance and tickets have run out, you can still visit the Generalife and gardens. The Palacios Nazaríes are also open for night visits (🕐 22.00–23.30 Tues–Sat (Mar–Oct); 20.00–21.30 Fri & Sat (Nov–Feb)). Advance tickets can be collected at the ticket offices or the automatic machines located in the Access Pavilion, situated by the main car park. You'll need your printed reservation slip or booking reference number and the credit card used to book the tickets. You can buy a maximum of five tickets at one time. Ⓝ Minibus: 30 or 32 from Plaza Nueva

SIGHTS & ATTRACTIONS

Puerta de la Justicia (Gate of Justice)

From the ticket office, visitors are guided along a broad path inside the Alhambra's walls, but a more interesting route is to go down the road, following the outside of the walls. Ignore the first road to the right and you will come to a bend over which looms the monumental portal of the Gate of Justice, a traditional entrance to the fortress with a staggered path through it to deter invaders. There are two carvings on the outer wall of the gate: a hand (on the taller, outer horseshoe arch) and, lower down, a key with a tassel attached to it. These symbols have never been explained.

Alcazaba

The ramp from the Puerta de la Justicia brings you into the Plaza de los Aljibes (Square of the Cisterns), one side of which is formed by the Alcazaba, the oldest part of the Alhambra, which probably stands on Roman foundations. An austere fortress of walls and six towers, the Alcazaba tapers towards the apex of the hill where the Torre de la Vela (Watchtower) stands guard over the city below. It offers tremendous views from its battlements over Granada's rooftops, across the ravine to the Albaicín and south to the Sierra Nevada.

Palacios Nazaríes (Nasrid Palaces)

The finest part of the Alhambra is the complex of royal (or Nasrid) palaces. There may have been as many as seven palaces in the Alhambra's heyday, but now there are essentially three interlocking suites of magnificently decorated chambers and delightful patios.

The first part of the palaces is the Mexuar, which has one open and one enclosed courtyard. This part of the Alhambra was much altered by Granada's Christian conquerors and so is not in its original state. Its main two rooms are the Hall of the Mexuar, probably used as a council chamber but later converted into a chapel, and the Golden Chamber, which, despite its suggestive name, may have been a mere waiting room for those about to have an audience with the king.

From the Mexuar you step into the long rectangular patio of the Palacio de Comares, which is known as the Patio de los Arrayanes (Courtyard of the Myrtles) because of the hedges planted beside its central pool.

At the northern end of this pond is the chamber which makes the greatest impression on visitors, the Salón de Embajadores (Hall of the Ambassadors), also called the Throne Room. The ceiling of the chamber is made of more than 8,000 separate pieces of coloured wood.

A humble doorway leads from the Comares patio to the exquisite Patio de los Leones (Courtyard of the Lions), a cloister of slender columns and beautiful filigree decorations. The namesake lions have undergone extensive renovation and are on display with explanation plaques in an exhibition room off the courtyard. Also off the courtyard are the splendidly ornate Sala de los Reyes (Hall of the Kings), Sala de las Dos Hermanas (Hall of the Two Sisters) and Sala de los Abencerrajes (Hall of the Abencerrajes). This last has a star-shaped cupola dripping with *mocarabes* – stalactite stucco mouldings that are supposed to recall the cave in which Muhammad received his inspiration for the Koran. There are supposedly irremovable stains of blood in the floor/fountain of the Hall of the Abencerrajes, as evidence of the murder of members of one clan by another, but these are merely reddish veins in the marble.

You leave the rooms occupied by Washington Irving and pass through two courtyards that were added to the Alhambra in the 16th century. Off the second courtyard is the palace bathhouse, which is lit by star-shaped holes in the ceiling and has some surviving tilework on the walls.

Partal & the Medina

The area behind the Palacio de los Leones is called the Partal and its most notable feature is the Torre de las Damas (Tower of the Ladies), which is little more than a portico standing beside a large pond. Paths lead from here past several towers along the Alhambra's northern walls towards the entrance to the Generalife. The best way to return from the Generalife is via the broad path from the ticket office, which passes the ruins of the Medina, once a city of courtiers' palaces and the houses of soldiers and servants.

Generalife

The Alhambra may look like the sort of luxurious residence a sultan would never want to leave, but he also had a second home further up the hill, the Generalife, which was far enough away from his daily work of running the kingdom for him to be able to relax, but still close enough to be able to attend to any urgent affairs of state. In front of the palace is a very long, much-photographed pond with twin rows of fountains feeding it. Around the palace are extensive formal gardens, although most of what you see is the result of rebuilding and reshaping according to modern tastes. The most unusual feature is the Escalera del Agua (Water Staircase), in which a stream is ingeniously divided and fed, gurgling down the two handrails.

CULTURE

Palacio de Carlos V

In 1626 Spain's King Carlos I (better known as Holy Roman Emperor Charles V) ordered the construction of a palace within the walls of the Alhambra, which involved the demolition of some existing buildings. Anywhere else and it would have to be considered as one of the greatest works of the Spanish Renaissance, but it is undeniably out of character here and put into the aesthetic shade by the Moorish palaces next door. The palace is visited separately from the Alhambra. It contains two museums: the Museo de la Alhambra, which displays works of Islamic art, and the Museo de Bellas Artes (Museum of Fine Art). Next to the palace is a church and a small but pleasing bathhouse.

Museo de la Alhambra ☎ (958) 027 900 ⓦ www.juntade andalucia.es/cultura/museos/MBAGR ⏱ 14.30–20.00 Tues, 09.00–20.00 Wed–Sat, 09.00–14.30 Sun (summer); 14.30–18.00 Tues, 09.00–18.00 Wed–Sat, 09.00–14.30 Sun (winter)

🔺 *Visit the museums of the Palacio de Carlos V*

Museo de Bellas Artes ☎ (958) 575 450 Ⓦ www.juntade
andalucia.es/cultura/museos/MBAGR ◷ 14.30–20.00 Tues,
09.00–20.00 Wed–Sat, 09.00–14.30 Sun (summer); 14.30–18.00
Tues, 09.00–18.00 Wed–Sat, 09.00–14.30 Sun (winter)
❶ Admission charge for non-EU citizens

RETAIL THERAPY

Cuesta de Gomérez The steep street heading up to the Alhambra
from Plaza Nueva is lined with mostly indifferent souvenir shops
specialising in ceramics and marquetry. It is a traditional location
for guitar workshops but only two are left (there are others
elsewhere in Granada): J Lopez (No 36) and Manuel Diaz (No 29).
One of the better craft/souvenir shops is **El Suspiro** (ⓐ Cuesta de
Gomérez 45 ☎ (958) 229 996 ◷ 11.00–20.30 daily), which has
Granada pottery and other items.

Laguna Taracea If you want to buy a serious piece of craftwork, step
into this marquetry shop that has been running since 1877. Some
of the items are still made on the premises using the same
techniques employed by 14th-century Granadino craftsmen.
ⓐ Calle Real de la Alhambra 30 ☎ (958) 229 019 Ⓦ www.laguna-
taracea.com ◷ 09.30–18.00 Mon–Fri, 09.30–13.30 Sat & Sun

Librería de la Alhambra There are three bookshops inside the
monument: the largest and most comprehensive is inside the
Palacio de Carlos V; another is by the ticket booths and the third
is in the old post office on Calle Real de la Alhambra. ☎ (954) 293 079
◷ 08.00–20.00 daily (summer); 08.00–18.30 daily (winter)

Ruiz Linares This large souvenir shop is often heaving with coach parties. ⓐ Calle Real de la Alhambra 64 ⓣ (958) 221 971 ⓦ www.anticuarioruizlinares.com ⓛ 09.30–17.30 Mon–Sat, 09.30–13.30 Sun

TAKING A BREAK

There aren't many places to eat within easy reach of the Alhambra. Your best bet is to either take a picnic with you (but don't eat it inside the Alhambra's grounds) or get back down to the Plaza Nueva, where there are endless bars and restaurants.

Alhambra Palace £££ ❶ A hotel across the hill from the Alhambra, with kitsch Moorish decoration. There are great views over the city from the bar's terrace, which is open to non-guests. ⓐ Plaza Arquitecto García de Paredes 1 ⓣ (958) 221 468 ⓦ www.h-alhambrapalace.es ⓛ Bar terrace: 11.00–23.00 daily; restaurant: 07.30–10.30, 13.00–15.00, 20.00–23.00 daily

⬥ Pottery, paintings and plenty more at El Suspiro

The city centre

A long broad street, Gran Vía de Colón, separates the Albaicín (see page 86) from the city centre. It meets the other principal street through the city, Calle Reyes Católicos, at Plaza Isabel la Católica. The angle between these is packed with small squares and narrow streets around the cathedral. Two larger squares, Plaza Bib-Rambla and Plaza Trinidad, provide relief from the mass of bars, shops and apartment blocks.

Across the other side of Reyes Católicos the streets behind the Plaza del Carmen (on which stands the town hall) lead towards the district of El Realejo. There are few sights to tempt you in this direction in the daytime, but plenty of bars that might attract you at night.

From Puerta Real, at the end of Reyes Católicos, the city centre continues down the busy streets of Recogidas (towards the inner ring road, the Camino Ronda) and the Acera del Darro (towards the banks of the Río Genil). Again, it won't be sightseeing that leads you down here, but bars and shops.

SIGHTS & ATTRACTIONS

Capilla Real (Royal Chapel)

The conquerors of Muslim Granada and unifiers of Spain, King Fernando and Queen Isabel, better known as the Reyes Católicos (Catholic Monarchs), are buried in this Gothic chapel especially built for the purpose. Although much smaller than the cathedral next door, it is far more interesting to visit. Steps take you down from the entrance hall (Lonja) into the chapel proper, which has

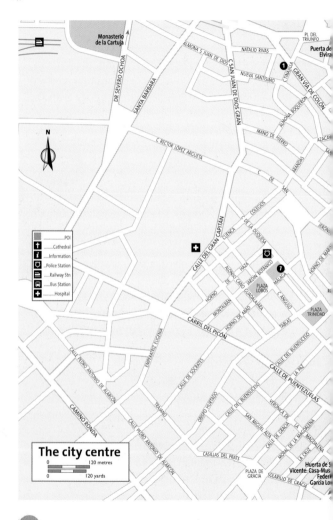

The city centre

0   120 metres

0   120 yards

Palacio de Dar Al-Horra

Monasterio de Sta Isabel la Real

ALBAICÍN

Convento de Sta Catalina de Zafra

Museo Arqueológico y Etnológico

Puente de Cadí

Real Chancilleria

Iglesia de Santa Ana

Alcazaba

GRAN VÍA DE COLÓN

Capilla Real

Cathedral of Granada

Palacio de la Madraza

Bosque de la Alhambra

Puerta de las Granadas

Fundación Rodríguez-Acosta

Centro de Arte Contemporáneo José Guerrero

Corral del Carbón

Museo de Artes y Costumbres Populares

EL REALEJO

Plaza Campo del Príncipe

Town Hall

PLAZA DEL CAMPILLO

SAN ANTÓN

SAN MATÍAS

JUANA LA LOCA

History hasn't been kind to Fernando and Isabel's daughter who is buried with them in the Capilla Real. She will forever be remembered by the unkind epithet of Juana la Loca (Joanna the Mad), although it is far from certain that she was actually insane. Lovesick and grief-stricken, certainly, which is a better explanation for her reckless behaviour. When her adored but serially unfaithful husband Felipe (Philip the Fair) died young, she set off with his body on a journey from Burgos in northern Spain to Granada, travelling by night and opening the coffin every now and then to gaze at his decomposing remains. She and her grisly cargo didn't reach Granada according to schedule, but they both ended up being buried here much later.

three impressively ornate iron grilles. Beyond the largest of these are two sepulchres, one for the Catholic Monarchs and one for their daughter, the unfortunately named Juana la Loca (Joanna the Mad), and her husband Felipe el Hermoso (Philip the Fair). A large altarpiece looks down on the sepulchres. Below ground is a crypt where the coffins of all four royals – together with that of an infant prince – reside. You leave the chapel through the sacristy, where primitive Flemish art is on display alongside Fernando's sword and Isabel's crown.

ⓐ Calle Oficios ⓣ (958) 229 239 ⓦ www.capillarealgranada.com
ⓛ 10.15–13.30, 16.00–19.30 Mon–Sat, 11.00–13.30, 15.30–19.30
Sun ⓘ Admission charge

Casa de los Tiros: Museo de Artes y Costumbres Populares (House of Shots Folk Museum)

You might just want to admire this 16th-century mansion from the outside, as the façade is a delightful bit of restrained Gothic, with the figures of five Greek heroes embedded in it. It's said to get its popular name – 'the House of Shots' – from the cannons that protrude from the battlements at the top of the façade, but a legend (wholly without foundation) has a more colourful explanation. In 1723 the Marquis of El Salar ran a young student through with his sword in a duel after the latter had offended the lady with whom he was in love. Rather than face the dishonour of trial and execution, the marquis shut himself up in this house and shot himself twice. The next day a letter arrived saying that he was to be pardoned for his crime, but it was, of course, too late. Exactly 100 years later an inhabitant of the house is said to have knocked down a hollow-sounding wall and stumbled into the very room where the marquis had taken his own life.

However it got its nickname, the building is now officially a museum dealing with the history of Granada. Among the exhibits there's a fascinating map dated 1796, which is effectively an A–Z guide to the pre-industrial city. Room 4, meanwhile, deals with 19th-century Romantic travellers, including Washington Irving (see page 62). ⓐ Calle Pavaneras 19 ⓣ (958) 575 466 ⓛ 14.30–20.30 Tues, 09.00–20.30 Wed–Sat, 09.00–14.30 Sun ❶ Admission charge for non-EU citizens

Catedral de Granada (Granada Cathedral)

Granada's central church was begun on the site of the city's main mosque shortly after the Reconquest. It is considered a prime example of Spanish Renaissance architecture but is more impressive outside than it is inside, and if you are pressed for time, or don't care for too many churches, see the Capilla Real next door instead.

It officially stands on the Gran Vía de Colón, but you could walk past it unless you were looking for the wrought-iron gateway leading to it. Curiously, its main façade looks the other way, on to an inconspicuous pedestrianised square off the corner of the more expansive Plaza Bib-Rambla.

The most impressive thing about the interior is its immense volume, which is divided into a nave and four aisles by stout white columns. Various artistic treasures are distributed around the building including 16th-century Flemish stained-glass windows

◆ *The magnificent Catedral and Capilla Real*

depicting the Passion, two life-sized coloured statues of Fernando and Isabel (the Catholic Monarchs) kneeling in pious prayer, golden statues of the Apostles, a statue of St James on horseback, a superb Late Gothic doorway and many large paintings by Juan de Sevilla, Alonso Cano and others. ⓐ Gran Vía de Colón (entrance on Calle Oficios) ❶ (958) 222 959 ⏰ 10.45–13.30, 16.00–20.00 Mon–Sat, 16.00–20.00 Sun (summer); 10.45–13.30, 16.00–19.00 Mon–Sat, 16.00–19.00 Sun (winter) ❶ Admission charge. Around the cathedral and Capilla Real you may be approached by one of several gypsy women who make a living out of thrusting sprigs of rosemary into the hands of unwary visitors, telling them it is a gift. If you accept the rosemary, the woman will insist on telling your fortune and demand payment. If you are not in the mood, politely decline the rosemary and keep walking.

Corral del Carbón (Coal House)

This 14th-century Arab caravanserai is the only such building surviving in Spain. It was originally an inn and warehouse for travelling merchants but was turned into a charcoal burners' depot – hence the name – and, in the 16th century, into a theatre. In some ways it is this last use that suits it best and it is still used as an occasional venue for summer concerts. From the street an impressive horseshoe-arched gateway lets you through into a courtyard of three storeys of galleries looking down on a small fountain. It's a peaceful corner of the city – only a step away from the busy Calle Reyes Católicos – now home to government offices. ⓐ Calle Mariana Pineda ❶ (958) 221 144 ⏰ 10.30–13.30, 17.00–20.00 Mon–Fri, 10.30–14.00 Sat

Huerta de San Vicente: Casa-Museo Federico García Lorca (San Vicente Gardens: House & Museum of Federico García Lorca)

The house where the poet and playwright Federico García Lorca (see box, page 20) spent his summers and wrote some of his best-loved pieces, including the play *Blood Wedding*, used to be 2 km (1¼ miles) outside the city but now stands in its own park between Calle Arabial and the ring road. Visitors are taken on a 30-minute guided tour, which explains Lorca's life and work.
ⓐ Calle Virgen Blanca ⓣ (958) 258 466 ⓦ www.huertadesan vicente.com ⓛ 10.00–14.30 Tues–Sun (July & Aug); 10.00–12.30, 18.00–19.30 Tues–Sun (Apr–June & Sept); 10.00–12.30, 16.00–18.30 Tues–Sun (Oct–Mar) ⓘ Admission charge

Monasterio de la Cartuja

It's only worth making the trek out to this 16th- to 17th-century monastery if you have a taste for the excesses of Baroque decoration. If you have, you will love the florid white stucco in the church and sacristy, which are considered among the finest examples of Churrigueresque – an extreme version of Baroque.
ⓐ Paseo de Cartuja ⓣ (958) 161 932 ⓛ 10.00–13.00, 16.00–20.00 daily (summer); 10.00–13.00, 15.00–18.00 daily (winter) ⓝ Bus: 8
ⓘ Admission charge

Plaza Bib-Rambla

This large rectangular square occupies the former site of an old Arab gateway. Shaded by lime trees and with a daily flower market, it is a pleasant space to take a break from shopping. There are bars and cafés here, with tables set out on the pavements, some of them serving *chocolate con churros* (hot

⬤ *Find a shady spot to cool down in the Plaza Bib-Rambla*

chocolate and batter sticks to dunk), which are eaten for breakfast, as a snack in the evening, or, during fiestas, at just about any time of the day or night. In the middle of the square is a fountain taken from a demolished convent, which rests on the shoulders of four grotesque giants.

Plaza Isabel la Católica

This square is the closest thing Granada has to a central focal point, but it's not an inviting place to hang around. It is named after the queen of Castile who, along with her husband Fernando, captured Granada from the Moors in 1492. The statue in the middle of the square is a 19th-century work by Mariano Benillure, and it shows Isabel with that other protagonist of the year 1492, Christopher Columbus (Cristóbal Colón in Spanish).

El Realejo

This area is sometimes described as the former Jewish quarter of the city, but there is no evidence for it having been so. In 1497 the city council ordered a swathe of streets and houses to be flattened to form the Plaza Campo del Príncipe (around which it is grouped) in honour of the marriage of the heir apparent in that year. Sadly, he died six months after the marriage. The square is now a centre for bars and clubs. The only other reason to stray this way is if you want to go up to or come down from the Alhambra on foot following a quieter route than the Cuesta de Gomérez from Plaza Nueva. On the way you might want to stop and look at the former residence of the Granada-born painter José María Rodríguez-Acosta (1878–1941). The house is in a straight white modern style set off by cypress trees, but the artist accessorised it with an eclectic selection of historical artefacts (some genuine, others imitation).

Fundación Rodríguez-Acosta ⓐ Callejón Niño del Rollo 8
ⓣ (958) 227 497 ⓦ www.fundacionrodriguezacosta.com
ⓛ By appointment only ⓘ Admission charge

CULTURE

Centro de Arte Contemporáneo José Guerrero (José Guerrero Centre of Contemporary Art)

This contemporary art gallery always has one room dedicated to the paintings of the Granada-born abstract artist (1914–91) after whom it is named, but the other two main rooms and smaller spaces are dedicated to changing exhibitions of avant-garde installations, including multimedia shows. ⓐ Calle Oficios 8

> **CHRISTOPHER COLUMBUS**
> Columbus 'sailed the ocean blue in fourteen hundred and ninety-two', but he wouldn't have done so had events the year before gone another way. It was during the protracted siege of Granada that the Genoese adventurer relentlessly importuned the queen for funds to make his voyage. He'd all but given up hope when she finally agreed to commission him. One story has it that she pawned her jewels to subsidise his three-piece fleet, but it is fairly certain she didn't do so until she was sure that the rich prize of Granada was about to fall into her hands.

☎ (958) 225 185 ⓦ www.centroguerrero.org ⏱ 10.30–14.00, 16.00–21.00 Tues–Sat, 10.30–14.00 Sun

Palacio de la Madraza

Although this building across the street from the cathedral and the Capilla Real has an 18th-century façade, it is actually much older. It was originally built in the 14th century as a school for Koranic studies and, although it has been much altered since the Reconquest, it still has its original hall and *mihrab* (prayer niche). It is mainly used for artistic and cultural events. ⓐ Calle Oficios 14 ⏱ Closed for restoration until mid-2011

RETAIL THERAPY

Alcaicería This 19th-century re-creation of the city's Arab silk bazaar conjures a faux oriental feel and is an inviting place to shop, but don't expect to find too many authentic Granadino crafts for sale as most of the items are souvenirs for tourists. One of the better shops inside it is **Artesanía Alcaicería** (ⓐ Stalls 1, 3 and 10 ☎ (958) 229 045 ⓦ www.alcaiceria.com), which specialises in miniature figures for Christmas cribs.

Metro International Bookshop This shop has the best stock of English books in Granada. ⓐ Calle de Gracia 31 (between Calle de Puentezuelas and Plaza de Gracia) ☎ (958) 261 565 ⏱ 10.00–14.00, 17.00–20.30 Mon–Fri, 11.00–14.00 Sat

La Oliva This is a great shop for olive oil aficionados, with a superb range of top-quality extra virgin olive oils – including organic – as well as related products such as soaps. Tastings are also offered. ⓐ Calle Rosario (off Calle Varela) ⓣ (958) 225 754 ⓛ 10.00–14.00, 17.00–20.00 daily

TAKING A BREAK

Bodega Espadafor £ ❶ An old-fashioned bar that's well known for its tapas. ⓐ Calle Tinajilla ⓣ (958) 202 138 ⓛ 12.00–16.00, 20.00–24.00 Mon–Sat

Bodegas Casteñeda £ ❷ A typical bodega with dark wood furniture and beams. The superb tapas on offer include cured cheese in olive oil and a deliciously moist tortilla served with garlic-spiked mayonnaise. There is an excellent selection of wines. ⓐ Calle Almireceros 1–3 (off Gran Vía de Colón) ⓣ (958) 223 222 ⓛ 11.00–24.00 daily

○ *Lose yourself in the alleyways of the Alcaicería*

Café Fútbol £ ❸ This bar-restaurant with terrace is famous for ice creams and *chocolate con churros*. ⓐ Plaza Mariana Pineda 6 ⓣ (958) 226 662 ⓛ 06.00–24.00 Mon–Fri, 06.00–02.00 Sat & Sun

Los Diamantes £ ❹ It certainly doesn't look like anything special, but the three-deep crowd at the bar should tell you otherwise. The free tapas are legendary and if you drink your way through enough beers, the accompanying parade of free delicacies might include anything from garlic prawns to deep-fried tempura-style slices of aubergine. ⓐ Calle Navas 28 ⓣ (958) 227 070 ⓛ 13.00–16.00, 20.00–22.30 Tues–Sat (Oct–Aug)

Vía Colón £ ❺ The Baroque mouldings and marble counter tops may be imitation old but this is still a lovely place for a sandwich or lunch. Not a relaxing place to linger too long but it does have a terrace outside in summer. ⓐ Gran Vía de Colón 13 ⓣ (958) 220 752 ⓛ 09.00–24.00 Mon–Thur & Sun, 09.00–00.30 Fri & Sat

Taberna Casa Enrique ££ ❻ A classic near Puerta Real serving good tapas and a choice of wines. ⓐ Acera del Darro 8 ⓣ (958) 255 008 ⓛ 12.00–16.00, 20.00–24.00 Mon–Sat

AFTER DARK

RESTAURANTS
Botánico £ ❼ A cool, modern restaurant where the menu combines food from Mexico, North Africa and Asia. ⓐ Calle Málaga 3 ⓣ (958) 271 598 ⓛ 13.00–00.30 Mon–Thur & Sun, 13.00–01.30 Fri & Sat

Chikito ££ ❽ Creative Andalucían cooking in this traditional restaurant and bar set in a lovely square. ⓐ Plaza del Campillo 9 ❶ (958) 223 364 Ⓦ www.restaurantechikito.com ❺ 13.00–16.00, 20.00–23.30 Thur–Tues

Cunini ££ ❾ This inviting wood-panelled restaurant serves arguably the best seafood in town, with the day's catch on display in the window. The fried fish or *caldereta* (rice and seafood stew) are good options. ⓐ Calle Pescadería 14 (off Alcaicería) ❶ (958) 250 777 ❺ 13.00–16.00, 20.00–23.30 Tues–Sat, 13.00–16.00 Sun

Sevilla £££ ❿ One of Federico García Lorca's favourite restaurants, opposite the Capilla Real and serving traditional Andalucían dishes. ⓐ Calle Oficios 12 ❶ (958) 221 223 Ⓦ www.restaurantesevilla.es ❺ 13.00–16.00, 20.00–23.30 Tues–Sat, 13.00–16.00 Sun

LIVE MUSIC

El Eshavira This is a suitably moody, dimly lit club north of the cathedral where you can hear live blues and jazz, and occasional flamenco. For more flamenco the best area is the Albaicín and Sacromonte (see page 100). ⓐ Calle Postigo de la Cuna 2 (off Gran Vía de Colón) ❶ (958) 290 829 ❺ 22.00–03.30 Tues–Sat

CLUBS

Granada 10 A cinema in the evening; a discotheque at night (from 00.30 to 06.00 on weekdays and 07.00 at weekends) playing disco, hip hop, funk, Latin, salsa – you name it. ⓐ Calle de la Cárcel Baja 10 ❶ (958) 224 001

The Albaicín & Sacromonte

Two hills face each other across the narrow valley of the River Darro. On one stands the Alhambra; the other is occupied by the Albaicín (sometimes spelt Albayzin), the most perfectly preserved Moorish quarter in Spain. Because of the terrain it is built on, the Albaicín is characterised by narrow streets, which are usually steep and often stepped – many are called *cuesta* (meaning slope).

Most of the charm here is in wandering around and seeing what you stumble on by chance. You won't be able to miss the churches, as their bell towers (barely disguised minarets) stand proud above all other buildings. Also conspicuous (but secretive at the same time) are the *carmines* – the typical well-to-do houses of the Albaicín, which are villas with gardens protected by high walls. Most of them you can only glimpse through their gates, but some have been put to public use as restaurants and the like. Other features to look out for are the innumerable water cisterns, *aljibes*, which are organised according to an ingenious 500-year-old water-supply system.

The Albaicín is worth a leisurely visit in its own right, but it also offers the best views of the Alhambra, particularly from the Plaza (or Mirador de) San Nicolás outside the church of the same name. At a push you can get from the city centre to this viewpoint and back in an hour, but it would be a shame to rush it and it is certainly a good idea to allow yourself time in case you get lost (very likely) and need to find your bearings again.

There are many ways into the Albaicín, but the most popular is to take Calderería Nueva from Calle de Elvira (near the corner of Plaza Nueva), which brings you to Plaza San Gregorio. If you keep climbing in the same direction and bear uphill to your left, you will eventually strike the Plaza San Nicolás.

A more interesting route is to turn left almost immediately after leaving Plaza San Gregorio up Grifos de San José. Veer left at the end and you will be in Placeta de San José, which is overlooked by a delightful 10th-century minaret. Go uphill underneath the minaret and you'll reach the pretty Plaza de San Miguel Bajo. From here it is a straight run along Calle de Santa Isabel La Real, past the 16th- to 17th-century convent of the same name (for visits, call ☎ (958) 200 688), to San Nicolás.

From Plaza San Nicolás all roads lead down to the Darro valley. If you get lost, face the Alhambra, which is visible from almost everywhere, and head downhill. This way you will strike one of Granada's most historic streets, the Carrera del Darro. Turn right and you will come to Plaza Nueva.

Beyond the Albaicín is Sacromonte, the old gypsy quarter of the city where many people still live, by choice, in caves carved out of the soft rock. There is an excellent visitor centre explaining cave life and the traditions (including flamenco music and dance) of Sacromonte.

SIGHTS & ATTRACTIONS

El Bañuelo

There's not much to see from outside unfortunately, but this Arab bath has a fine vaulted interior lit by star-shaped apertures in the ceiling. These baths were built in the 11th century and are therefore older than most of the Alhambra. The main chamber has incongruous columns supporting carved capitals that were

The Albaicín & Sacromonte

0 ——— 90 metres
0 ——— 90 yards

Sala Albayzin

CARRETERA DE MURCIA

PLTA ALMONA

PL AUIATAR

PT LARGA

CENICEROS

VEREDILLAS DE S. CRISTOBAL

BAJO S. ILDEFONSO

Arco de las Pesas

CUESTA ALHACABA

PTA DE LAS MINAS

ALGIBE DE LA GITANA

PL DEL TRIUNFO

Puerta de Elvira

CTA ABARQUEROS

Palacio de Dar Al-Horra

CJON CAMPANAS

PL SAN NICOLAS

Mezquita Mayor ❼

CTRA. MARÍA DE LA MIEL

SAN NICOLAS

LAS MONJAS

PILAR SECO

C NUEVO DE SAN NII

CARRIL DE LA LONA

CIÓN

❶ **Monasterio de Sta Isabel la Real**

ZENETE

CALLE DE SANTA ISABEL LA REAL

GUMIEL S. JOSE

ALGIBE DE TRILL

PL DE SAN MIGUEL BAJO

CRUZ DE QUIROS

SAN JOSE

SAN JOSE INN

CLAVEL

CALLEJON DEL ALGIBE DE TRILLO

CALLE DE ELVIRA

BOCANEGRA

QUIADA

CARRO CLAVEL

AZACAYAS

CTA DE LA BAñEZA

CUESTA MARAÑAS

PLTA DE SAN JOSE

S TRES

❷

CTA DE LA LONA

PL SAN GREGORIO

GRUPO DE SAN JOSE

S GREGORIO

Iglesia de Santa Ana

GRAN VIA DE COLON

AZACAYAS

SANTA PAULA

CALLE DE ELVIRA

❻

PL STA ANA

CARCEL ALTA

GRAN VIA DE COLON

CALDERERIA NUEVA

Real Chancillería ℹ

HOSPITAL DE SANTA ANA

TINDILLAS STA PAULA MARQUES

SANTA PAULA

❹

CALDERERIA VIEJA

❺

CARCEL BAJA

CALLE DE ELVIRA

C DE SAN JERONIMO

CETTI MERIEM

JOAQUIN

PLAZA NUEVA

SAN AGUSTIN

ALMIRECEROS

HORNO DE MARINA

COSTA

🚌

COLCHA

Capilla Real ✝

PL CUCHILLEROS

brought from elsewhere, possibly from Córdoba. ⓐ Carrera del Darro 31 ⓣ (958) 229 738 ⓛ 09.30–14.00 Tues–Sat

Calle de Elvira & Puerta de Elvira

The narrow, winding Calle de Elvira shadows the Gran Vía de Colón from Plaza Nueva to Plaza del Triunfo: the one a distinctly indirect oriental route; the other a no-nonsense, broad, modern avenue. Guarding the Plaza del Triunfo end of the street is the Puerta de Elvira, which was the main entrance through the walls of the Albaicín. Sadly, bits of it were progressively removed after the Reconquest until only the outer part was left.

Carrera del Darro

The Carrera del Darro runs along the valley of the River Darro, which separates the Alhambra from the Albaicín. There are

◒ *The star-shaped vents inside El Bañuelo*

terrace bars and various historic buildings along the way, including El Bañuelo, the Museo Arqueológico y Etnológico and two convents. Hovering over the river is an impressive 11th-century half-arch, the Puente de Cadí or Puerta de los Tableros, which is thought to have been part of both a dam and a military route between the Alhambra and Albaicín.

Plaza Larga

The focal point of the upper Albaicín is this square, which is home to a daily market. A small dog-legged gateway, the Arco de las Pesas (Arch of the Weights), connects it with the unnoticeable Placeta de las Minas. The name is thought to have been bestowed on it because the fraudulent weights of unscrupulous traders were hung here as an example to others.

Plaza Nueva

Unlike most other Spanish cities, Granada hasn't got a single main square or *plaza mayor* around which the layout of the city revolves. This elongated space between the Alhambra and the Albaicín, however, shares the function with the adjacent Plaza Isabel la Católica. It is really three squares in one, with Plaza Santa Ana joined to its top end (looked down on by a Moorish-style church of the same name) and Plaza Cuchilleros stuck on to it at the bottom. Three important roads meet here: the narrow and winding road of Calle de Elvira, the Carrera del Darro and the Cuesta de Gomérez, which ascends towards the Alhambra. The city's main tourist office is off the corner of the square near the church. The most conspicuous building on Plaza Nueva is the 16th-century Real Chancillería (Royal Chancery) or law courts.

Plaza San Nicolás

The Mirador at the Plaza San Nicolás offers the classic view of the Alhambra with the (usually) snow-capped Sierra Nevada as a background. The church after which it is named stands in the middle of the square on the former site of one of the Albaicín's main mosques. Beside it now stands the Mezquita Mayor, a mosque serving Granada's latter-day Muslim community.

Mezquita Mayor 🕐 10.00–14.00, 18.00–21.00 daily (summer); 10.00–14.00, 15.00–19.00 daily (winter), but times may change during Muslim festivals

Sacromonte

Granada's 'Holy Mount' received its name after the Reconquest, largely because of several lead 'books' supposedly found in a cave at the end of the 16th century. Written in Arabic, they related the martyrdom of the apocryphal St Cecil (San Cecilio), first bishop of Granada, who lived during Roman times, but they were eventually judged to be fakes. However, an abbey (*abadía*) was built in the 17th century, which became a focal point of the Counter-Reformation in Andalucía. Beneath it are the catacombs where St Cecil is said to have been martyred.

Today, Sacromonte is better known as Granada's cave and gypsy quarter and the place to go to see and hear flamenco. Whatever draws you this way, you will certainly find a quarter of the city very different from all others, and the best place to learn about its life and traditions is the Museo Cuevas del Sacromonte, a complex of caves and gardens with displays on how people have traditionally lived and worked in Sacromonte, as well as folk art displays. Art exhibitions and flamenco shows take place here in the summer. If all this just whets your appetite, you can always stay in a cave yourself (see page 38).

🚌 Bus: 34 leaves from Plaza Nueva every hour

Abadía de Sacromonte underground cave chapels 🅐 Camino del Sacromonte 📞 (958) 221 445 🕐 By on-the-hour guided tours only 11.00–13.00, 16.00–18.00 Tues–Sun ❶ Admission charge

Museo Cuevas del Sacromonte 🅐 Barranco de los Negros 📞 (958) 215 120 🌐 www.sacromontegranada.com 🕐 10.00–14.00, 17.00–21.00 Tues–Sun (summer); 10.00–14.00, 16.00–19.00 Tues–Sun (winter) ❶ Admission charge

THE RETURN OF ISLAM

After the Reconquest of Spain, the new Christian rulers did their best to rid themselves of all remaining Muslims within their realm, despite the promises they had sworn to leave them in peace. By the early 17th century the last Muslims had been either driven into exile or forced to convert, and Spain was officially a 100 per cent Catholic country. And so things stayed until more tolerant times arrived. No sooner was Franco dead and the transition to democracy in progress than Muslims began to re-establish themselves in Spain, particularly in Granada. The first small communities were of converts to Islam, Spanish nationals who had adopted the faith. Spain's modern Muslims claim (with some justification) that they are not practitioners of an alien religion but the heirs to their co-religionists who had lived in Granada for generations before the arrival of the Catholic Monarchs.

CULTURE

Museo Arqueológico y Etnológico (Archaeological & Ethnological Museum)

A handsome Renaissance building with plateresque portal and magnificent staircase serves as Granada's small but interesting archaeology museum, with exhibits mainly from Roman times but also from the Iberians and Visigoths. ⓐ Casa de Castril, Carrera del Darro 43 ⓣ (958) 575 408 ⓛ 14.30–20.30 Tues, 09.00–20.30 Wed–Sat, 09.00–14.30 Sun ❶ Admission charge for non-EU citizens

Palacio de Dar Al-Horra

This house between Plaza de San Miguel Bajo and the walls of the Albaicín was built in the 15th century on the orders of the mother of Boabdil (see page 120). It is down a blind alleyway and it takes some finding, but it is worth the effort to get a more realistic idea of what buildings must have looked like in Muslim Granada. The Sala de la Reina (Queen's Room) has a beautiful gallery giving views over the back part of the Albaicín. At the top is a tower with even better views all round. ⓐ Callejón de las Monjas ⓣ (958) 027 811 ⓛ 10.00–14.00 Tues & Thur

RETAIL THERAPY

Alhacaba This ceramics shop near Plaza Larga also sells a few books and maps and usefully serves cold drinks. More prosaically, it has toilets for the use of customers. ⓐ Placeta Almona 2 ⓣ No phone ⓛ 09.30–13.30, 16.00–20.00 daily

○ *Plaza Nueva's Real Chancillería, built in the 16th century*

FLAMENCO

Flamenco is the music, song and dance of Andalucía, particularly of the gypsy community. You can see it and hear it at several places in Granada, particularly in the cave quarter of Sacromonte, which has its own dance variant, the *zambra*. Purists would say you have to be in the right place at the right time for a spontaneous performance of the real thing. Indeed, it is undeniable that most venues (*tablaos*) in Granada are geared up for tourists, but that shouldn't put you off if you enjoy it on the level of entertainment rather than sociology. The essence of flamenco is the rough wailing voice of the singer that

Al Sur de Granada All good, edible things made in the province of Granada are sold in this shop behind the Elvira gateway. Choice items include hams from Trevélez, cheeses (both goat's and sheep's), chestnut preserves and local wines. From 19.30 the shop turns into a bar. There are wine tastings held every Thursday evening at 19.00, and concerts are also occasionally staged downstairs. As a bonus you can book rural accommodation here and arrange walking and riding excursions. ⓐ Calle de Elvira 150 ⓣ (958) 270 245 ⓦ www.alsurde granada.net ⓛ 10.00–24.00 Mon–Sat, 10.00–16.00 Sun

Calderería Nueva This sloping pedestrianised street is like a slice of the East transplanted to Granada, a passageway through an oriental bazaar. It is lined with shops selling Arabic and North is often unaccompanied, except by rhythmic clapping. The rapid strumming of a guitar is often added. Songs are never less than full-on passionate and express a range of emotions – mainly sadness and torment. In true flamenco, neither the song nor the dance follows a prescribed script: they are never done the same way twice. The performer continues for as long as their emotions dictate and their stamina will allow. Flamenco is a living music form and several of today's leading exponents are more interested in exploring fusions between flamenco and other genres, such as jazz and rock, than clinging to a mythical purity from the past.

African crafts, and also with *teterías* (tea shops) with hookahs (water pipes) and a selection of teas.

Convento de San Bernardo Sweets are sold by the cloistered nuns of this convent via a turntable, and a selection of wines made in a monastery. ⓐ Calle de Gloria 1 ① (958) 227 892 ⓒ No specific time – when the door is open, go in and ring the bell

TAKING A BREAK

El Ají £ ❶ Grab a chair on the square and enjoy the delicious light eats served by this tempting restaurant and tapas bar. Try the barbecued chicken for a real taste-bud treat. ⓐ Plaza de San Miguel Bajo 9 ① (958) 292 930 ⓒ 08.00–22.00 Wed–Mon

La Fontana £ ❷ This welcoming bar in an old house with thick ochre-painted walls and iron-grilled windows manages to attract two different clienteles. In the afternoon it is a good place for a quiet coffee, but after dark it becomes a hip place to drink or play pool. ❸ Puente Cabreras, Carrera del Darro 19 ❶ (958) 227 759 ❷ 16.00–04.00 Fri & Sat, 16.00–03.00 Sun–Thur

El Pañero £ ❸ A lively and simple bar-restaurant that also has tables outside in the square. Dishes are large, hearty Granadino specialities. ❸ Plaza Aliatar 18 ❶ (958) 201 139 ❷ 12.30–17.00, 20.00–23.00 Mon, Tues, Thur & Fri, 12.30–23.00 Sat & Sun

▲ *The Alhambra could be the backdrop to your lunch*

Tetería Kasbah £ ❹ One of the largest, oldest and most inviting *teterías* on the street, the Kasbah serves a range of teas (some supposedly aphrodisiacal) as well as milkshakes, juices, wines and spirits and Arabic sweets. ⓐ Calderería Nueva 4 ❶ (958) 227 936 ⓛ 12.00–03.00 Sat, 12.00–01.30 Sun–Fri

AFTER DARK

RESTAURANTS

Pilar del Toro £ ❺ You can eat tapas in the bar or a full meal in the restaurant, but the really great pleasure here is sitting on the covered patio with a soothing drizzling fountain in the middle of it. ⓐ Calle Hospital de Santa Ana 12 ❶ (958) 225 470

Arrayanes ££ ❻ Providing authenticity after the faux-Moorish tea houses on Calderería Nueva, this venue serves excellent Moroccan cuisine including tagines and *harira* soup. No alcohol is served. ⓐ Cuesta Marañas 4 ❶ (958) 228 401 ⓦ www.rest-arrayanes.com ⓛ 13.30–16.30, 19.30–23.30 Wed–Mon

San Nicolás ££ ❼ A stunningly positioned restaurant just off the famous Mirador de San Nicolás, with views of the Alhambra from the upstairs dining room. The menu is all about innovative twists on traditional dishes, such as sautéed calamari with risotto. ⓐ Calle San Nicolás 3 ❶ (958) 804 262 ⓛ 13.00–17.00 Mon, 13.00–17.00, 20.00–23.00 Tues–Sun

Mirador de Aixa £££ ❽ A cosy and luxurious restaurant with an inventive take on traditional Granadino cuisine and a delightfully romantic terrace with tables overlooking the Alhambra. ⓐ Carril de San Agustín 2 ⓣ (958) 223 616 ⓦ www.miradordeaixa.com ⓛ 21.00–24.00 daily (summer); 13.30–15.30, 21.00–24.00 Tues–Sat, 13.30–15.30 Sun (winter)

FLAMENCO SHOWS

Peña Flamenca La Platería One for the true aficionados of flamenco, this historic *peña* (a kind of social club) is a meeting place and hangout for big local names in the flamenco scene. Shows are open to the public on Thursday nights at about 22.00 and are of reliably excellent quality. ⓐ Placeta de Toqueros 7 (off Calle Candil) ⓣ (958) 210 650 ⓦ www.laplateria.org.es ⓛ Opening times vary: check the website

Zambra La Rocío The chairs in this gypsy club are arranged in a circle around the performers so you always get a front-row seat. Shows begin nightly at around 22.00; if you call in advance or book through your hotel, there is also a minibus service which picks you up from your hotel and includes a short guided tour (in English, of a kind) of the Albaicín before the show. ⓐ Camino del Sacromonte 70 ⓣ (958) 121 183 ⓦ www.granadainfo.com/rocio

◗ *Andalucía's whitewashed houses are a delight*

OUT OF TOWN
trips

Beyond Granada

Granada has plenty to keep you occupied for a few days but it can also be used as a base for excursions to some other interesting places. Top of your list should be Córdoba with its fabulous mosque as a natural complement to a visit to the Alhambra. About the same distance away are the two beautiful Renaissance towns of Úbeda and Baeza. The ancient and monumental Antequera is slightly closer. Another day trip is to Málaga, a port city that is usually ignored by holidaymakers travelling to the Costa del Sol. It is worth a half-day's visit, especially if you like the work of Pablo Picasso, with a superb museum commemorating the city's prodigal son.

GETTING THERE

All the places mentioned in this chapter are reached from Granada by motorway or fast main road and can be visited on a day trip if you have your own transport, although an overnight stay is preferable. Except for Antequera, which is on the Granada to Algeciras railway line, the best way to get to all of them by public transport is to take a coach. The main bus company serving Andalucía is Alsina Graells (see page 49), which leaves from Granada's main bus station on Carretera de Jaén. Their buses to Baeza, Úbeda, Córdoba and Málaga all leave more or less hourly from around 8am to around 8pm. There is a train line from Granada to Córdoba that generally goes about twice a day, in the morning and the late afternoon.

SIGHTS & ATTRACTIONS

Antequera

This ancient town at the crossroads between Seville, Granada, Málaga and Córdoba has two clusters of monuments. One is uphill from the tourist information office through a formal

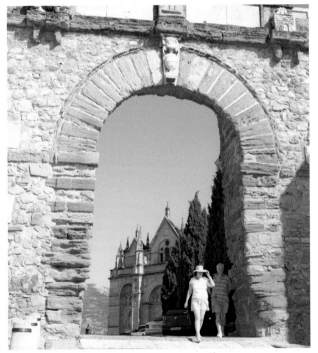

⬤ *Antequera's Arco de los Gigantes*

Granada region

0   18 km

0   12 miles

Übeda

aeza

Cazorla

JAÉN

Jódar

Huéscar

Pozo
Alcón

ampotéjar

Cúllar-Baza

Guadahortuna

A92

Sierra Arana

Baza

44

Serón

U   C   I   A

A92   Guadix   Sierra de Baza

GRANADA

GRANADA   Gérgal

44   Abrucena

Sierra Nevada   ALMERÍA

La Veleta   Mulhacén
3398   3481

rranco de   Bubión   Trevélez   Fondón
Poqueira

Capileira   Ugíjar   Sierra de Gádor

njarón   Alpujarras   Busquistar

Órgiva   Ferreirola   Berja   Almería

Pampaneira   Torvizcón

alobreña   Mecina   El Ejido
          Fondales

Motril   A7

Almuñécar

	City
	Large Town
	Small Town
	POI
	Main Road
	Minor Road
✈	Airport
	Railway
	Regional Border

Spain

Andalucía

N

16th-century gateway, the Arco de los Gigantes (Giants' Arch), and includes the Renaissance church of Real Colegiata de Santa María la Mayor and the remains of a Muslim fortress, the Alcazaba.

The other group of sights is on the edge of the town and far older than anything else you will see in Andalucía. The largest of Antequera's three prehistoric constructions (of unknown purpose) is the Dólmen de Menga, dating from 2500 BC, but the most interesting is the **Dólmen de Romeral**, which has a domed chamber – the first known case of intentional architectural construction in Europe.

Tourist information ⓐ Plaza San Sebastián 7 ⓣ (952) 708 142 ⓦ www.antequera.es

Dolmens ⓐ On the road out towards Archidona ⓛ 09.00–18.00 Tues–Sat, 09.30–14.30 Sun

Baeza & Úbeda

These two towns stand together on adjacent hills amid the olive groves of Jaén province. The smaller of the two is Baeza, which has a historic centre compact enough to stroll around in half an hour, but worth longer if you have the time. The place to start your tour is the immaculate Plaza del Pópulo just off the main square, the Plaza de la Constitución. Next to it are two gateways: the Puerta de Jaén and the Arco de Villalar. Head uphill from here to reach the cathedral, which looks across a square at a seminary on which students have left graffiti in elegant calligraphy. Downhill again and you come to the **Palacio de Jabalquinto**, famous for its Isabelline façade. On the other side of Plaza de la Constitución is one other building worth seeing, the Ayuntamiento (town hall), which once served as a prison.

The larger town of Úbeda is a museum of Renaissance architecture (once you have penetrated its modern suburbs). Many of its buildings are by the architect Andrés de Vandelvira, working for two nobles in the pay of the King of Spain, Francisco

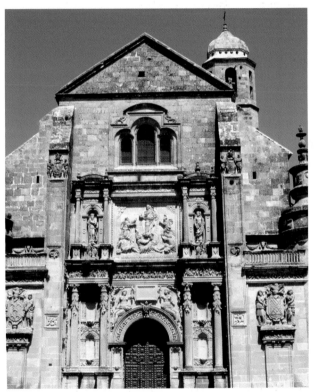

⬥ The church of El Salvador, on Úbeda's main square

de los Cobos and Juan Vázquez de Molina. Make straight for the Plaza de Vázquez de Molina, at the end of which stands the church of El Salvador, which has elaborate interior decoration. On the north side of the square is the former residence of the dean of Málaga, which is now a Parador hotel (you can step inside to see the patio), and the Palacio de las Cadenas, the town hall. Across the square are the Antiguo Pósito (a granary) and the church of Santa María de los Reales Alcázares. There are few buildings in Úbeda that are not ostentatiously Renaissance, but the finest of them is the **Iglesia de San Pablo**, built in the 13th century, which has one Gothic and one Romanesque door. Another is the 14th-century Casa Mudéjar, which houses Úbeda's archaeological museum.

Tourist information:

Baeza ⓐ Casa del Pópulo, Plaza del Pópulo ⓣ (953) 779 982 ⓦ www.baeza.es ⓛ 09.00–19.30 Mon–Fri, 09.30–15.00 Sat & Sun

Úbeda ⓐ Baja del Marqués 4 ⓣ (953) 779 204 ⓦ www.ubeda.es ⓛ 09.00–19.30 Mon–Fri, 09.30–15.00 Sat & Sun

Córdoba

Roman Córdoba was the capital of southern Spain and the birthplace of the poet Lucan and the philosopher Seneca. But it was after the Muslim invasion of Spain in the 8th century that it truly came into its own. In 929 Abd al-Rahman III declared himself caliph of Spain, with Córdoba as his capital. In the 10th and 11th centuries, while the rest of Europe was wallowing in a cultural dark ages, the civilised place to be was in Muslim Córdoba, where Christians and Jews were treated with tolerance, and art and learning thrived.

🔺 *Explore the old Jewish quarter of Córdoba*

The magnificence that once existed can today be seen in the famous **mosque** (*mezquita*) that dominates the city centre and is one of the key sights of Andalucía. It was built on the site of a Visigothic church and is the work of four caliphs. What impresses most is the immense size of the prayer hall, whose roof is supported by over 800 two-tier horseshoe arches rising from slender columns – many of which are recycled from Roman and Visigothic buildings. On the southern wall is a *mihrab* (prayer niche) decorated with intricate plasterwork and mosaics. When Córdoba was reconquered by the Christians, they couldn't leave such a structure untouched and in the 16th century a cathedral was dropped incongruously into the middle of it. The old minaret was simultaneously dressed up as a belfry.

For a more down-to-earth idea of medieval Córdoba, take a walk around the **Judería**, the old Jewish quarter of the city near the mosque. This is a delightful jumble of shady alleyways and whitewashed houses decorated with wrought-iron grilles and flowerpots. Many of them have secretive patios that are opened to the public in a special fiesta in early May. Look out for the **Sinagoga** (synagogue), no more than a delightful square hall with richly decorated walls, one of only three remaining in Spain.

There is just one drawback to visiting Córdoba: parking. If you are visiting for the day by car, the best policy is to head for the underground multi-storey car park on Avenida del Aeropuerto (which, as its name says, goes towards the airport), 15 minutes' walk from the monuments.

Outside Córdoba is **Madinat Al-Zahra**, a city built by caliph Abd al-Rahman III, which only survived 70 years before being ruined in a civil war. It is now the third-largest archaeological dig in Europe (after Pompeii and Knossos) but only a tenth of its ruins have so far been uncovered.

Tourist information ⓐ Calle Rey Heredia 22 ⓣ (957) 201 774 ⓦ www.turismodecordoba.org ⓛ 09.00–19.00 Mon–Fri, 10.00–19.30 Sat, 10.00–14.00 Sun

Mezquita ⓐ Calle de Torrijos ⓣ (957) 470 512 ⓛ 08.30–19.00 Mon–Sat, 08.30–10.00, 14.00–18.30 Sun ⓘ Admission charge but free 08.30–10.00 Mon–Fri

Sinagoga ⓐ Calle de los Judíos ⓣ (957) 202 928 ⓛ 09.30–14.00, 15.30–17.30 Tues–Sat, 09.30–13.30 Sun ⓘ Admission charge for non-EU citizens

Madinat Al-Zahra ⓐ 10 km (6 miles) west of Córdoba off the main A431, Km 6 road towards Palma del Río ⓣ (957) 355 506 ⓦ www.juntadeandalucia.es/cultura/museos/CAMA ⓛ 10.00–20.20 Tues–Sat, 10.00–14.00 Sun (summer); 10.00–18.30 Tues–Sat, 10.00–14.00 Sun (winter) ⓘ Admission charge for non-EU citizens

Málaga

Málaga's most important monument is the **Alcazaba**, a Moorish fortress entered through a series of horseshoe arches. Above it on the top of the hill is a castle of more recent construction, the **Gibralfaro**, which affords great views of the city. (To get to the latter, you might prefer to take the car to the top of the hill.)

Málaga makes great play of being Pablo Picasso's birthplace, even if the artist left when he was only ten years old and made his reputation elsewhere. The **Museo Picasso** displays a collection of 155 of his lesser works in a restored mansion,

● *Málaga's dramatic Muslim fortress, the Alcazaba*

which also has some superb 6th-century BC Phoenician ruins in its basement.

Alcazaba ⓐ Calle Alcazabilla ❶ No phone ● 09.30–20.00 daily (summer); 08.30–19.00 daily (winter) ❶ Admission charge

Gibralfaro ⓐ To get there by car follow the signs from Plaza del General Torrijos ❶ No phone ● 09.00–20.00 daily (summer); 09.00–18.00 daily (winter) ❷ Bus: 35 ❶ Admission charge

Museo Picasso ⓐ Palacio de Buenavista, Calle San Agustín 8 ❶ (902) 127 600 ⓦ www.museopicassomalaga.org ● 10.00–20.00 Tues–Thur & Sun, 10.00–21.00 Fri & Sat ❶ Admission charge but free on last Sun of month after 15.00

RETAIL THERAPY

Zoco El This pretty courtyard close to the synagogue in Córdoba is occupied by craftsmen and women who can be seen at work

in their studios. There's a shop selling their wares as you enter
from the street. ⓐ Calle de los Judíos, Córdoba

TAKING A BREAK

Los Dólmenes £ Straightforward place to eat local food.
For a starter, try Antequera's typical cold soup, *porra*.
ⓐ Cruz El Romeral, (next to the roundabout near Romeral
Dolmen), Antequera ⓣ (952) 845 956 ⓛ 13.00–16.00,
20.00–23.00 daily

Mesón Navarro £ A reasonably priced and very good menu
is served here, but there are also good tapas for a snack at any
time of day. ⓐ Plaza del Ayuntamiento 2, Úbeda ⓣ (953) 790 638
ⓛ 13.00–16.00, 20.00–23.00 daily

AFTER DARK

RESTAURANTS

Bodegas Campos £££ Wine bodega and fantastic restaurant.
A delightful place with excellent food. ⓐ Calle de Lineros 32,
Córdoba ⓣ (957) 497 500 ⓦ www.bodegascampos.com
ⓛ 13.30–16.00, 20.30–23.30 Mon–Fri, 13.30–16.00, 20.30–24.00
Sat & Sun

El Churrasco £££ The city's classic restaurant dispersed around
several patios and other pleasant dining spaces. Specialises
in grilled meats. ⓐ Calle Romero 16, Córdoba ⓣ (957) 290 819
ⓦ www.elchurrasco.com ⓛ 13.00–16.00, 20.30–24.00 daily

BARS & TAPAS

Taberna San Miguel £ Better known as 'El Pisto', a well-known old bar on a bullfighting theme where tapas are served along with Montilla-Moriles wines (the local equivalent of sherry). Plaza San Miguel 1, Córdoba (957) 470 166 12.00–16.00, 20.00–24.00 Mon–Sat, 12.00–16.00 Sun

FLAMENCO SHOWS

Tablao El Cardenal Flamenco show Mon–Sat at 22.30. Calle de Torrijos 10, Córdoba (957) 483 112 www.tablaocardenal.com

ACCOMMODATION

Maestre £ A hotel, *hostal* and set of one- or two-bedroom self-catering apartments close to the mosque, all of which are extremely good value for central Córdoba. Underground parking available. Calle Romero Barros 4–6, Córdoba (957) 472 410 www.hotelmaestre.com

Casa de los Naranjos ££ A small hotel with only 20 rooms in the old part of the city. Some of the furnishings were made by local craftsmen. Internet access available. Calle Isabel Losa 8, Córdoba (957) 470 587 www.casadelosnaranjos.com

Lola ££–£££ Any hotel that dares to advertise itself as 'the most beautiful hotel in Andalucía' must be worth taking a chance on. Each of the eight rooms is individually furnished with a touch of homeliness. The hotel is situated close to the mosque. Calle Romero 3, Córdoba (957) 200 305 www.hotellola.es

Granada province

Granada is the capital city of a small province of the same name, which offers a number of possible excursions. The two most popular trips are to the Alpujarras, over the other side of the Sierra Nevada, and down to the coast. Either can be done in a day, but you'll be much less stressed if you take two days or more, especially if you are travelling by public transport.

GETTING THERE

There are buses to the main towns and cities of the province, but the only way to see the countryside is by hire car. In winter you might be most tempted by the slopes of the Sierra Nevada, which offer skiing within easy reach of the city (see page 33).

SIGHTS & ATTRACTIONS

The Alpujarras & the Sierra Nevada

When the Moors were forced to leave Granada they found refuge not too far away in the valleys of the Alpujarras. They were not allowed to live in peace there for long, however, before being forced to choose between exile and conversion. The only traces of them today are in the architecture of the villages they left behind. For centuries life was hard in the Alpujarras and the people poor, but in recent decades the area has been 'discovered' by Spaniards and foreigners seeking a simpler life in the country – most famously the bestselling author Chris Stewart (see page 118).

The countryside of the Alpujarras is good walking and horse-trekking terrain and in spring and early summer is full of wild flowers, including many orchids.

Heading for the Alpujarras from Granada you pass first through Lanjarón – a spa town that distributes Andalucía's most popular brand of bottled water. The next town on the road is Órgiva, but you don't need to go into it. Instead, turn off just outside it on to the main road through the Alpujarras. Climbing up the valley and winding around the contours, this will bring you directly to the Barranco de Poqueira and three pretty villages. Lowest down,

�es *The lovely hillside villages of Bubión and Capileira*

and the first you reach, is Pampaneira. On the higher slopes are Bubión and Capileira. All three are built in the same way: a jumble of white houses with flat gravel roofs, each with an over-tall chimney rising out of it. Their streets are narrow, twisting, tapering and often stepped. Everywhere you look there are delightful details: porticoes, balconies and flowerpots.

Beyond Capileira, the mountains block communications to the north, except for a high-level road across the Sierra Nevada from Capileira to the ski resort (see page 33) on the other side. From spring to autumn, you can take a shuttle bus, organised by the national park, up part of this road from the Sierra Nevada National Park's Hoya del Portillo checkpoint above Capileira. This takes you close to La Veleta (3,398 m/11,148 ft) and Mulhacén (3,481 m/11,421 ft). The Sierra Nevada is the second-highest mountain chain in Europe after the Alps, and its highest parts have only sparse, hardy vegetation. (You can also get up to the heights of the Sierra Nevada by shuttle bus from the Hoya de la Mora National Park checkpoint above the ski resort, which is much closer to Granada.)

GERALD BRENAN & CHRIS STEWART

No one much beyond Granada had heard of the poor, backward Alpujarras before an Englishman, Gerald Brenan, installed himself there after fighting in World War I. He wrote about his experiences in a classic travel book, *South from Granada*. Among the visitors to his remote southern hideout were Virginia Woolf and fellow Bloomsbury Group member Lytton Strachey (who found that olive oil caused him indigestion and riding a mule played havoc with his piles). Sadly, there is nothing to see in Brenan's adoptive village of Yegen except a dull plaque on a wall. Decades later the Alpujarras were back on bookshelves everywhere with the success of *Driving Over Lemons*, and its subsequent sequels, by sometime Genesis drummer turned sheep-shearer, Chris Stewart. As with many other like-minded people from Spain and abroad, Stewart has chosen to settle in the Alpujarras because of the quality of life it offers and he writes about it with knowledge, humour and affection.

The main road through the Alpujarras continues to wriggle around the mountainsides from the Poqueira valley eastwards and there are more villages to see along the way both on and off it. Two pretty places a short way down the slope are Mecina Fondales and Ferreirola.

By the time you have got to Trevélez, Spain's highest town, at an altitude of 1,476 m (4,843 ft), where hams are cured in the dry mountain air, you've seen the best of the scenery. Your only options are to double back or go on a bit further and make a round trip by taking a right turning south to get back to Órgiva, via the small wine town of Torvizcón. A more arduous route is to cross the Sierra Nevada over its only pass, the Puerto de la Ragua, and pick up the motorway back to Granada from Guadix, but it's a long car journey with lots of curves.

Sierra Nevada National Park shuttle bus ☎ (630) 959 739

Costa Tropical (Tropical Coast)

Granada province's short shoreline is the most attractive stretch of Spain's southern Mediterranean coast and is only about an hour's drive from the city, making it theoretically possible to combine a day's sunbathing with a visit to the Alhambra, or even to fit in skiing and swimming in the sea on the same day!

The name 'Tropical Coast' comes from the many fruit orchards that extend up the valleys behind the coastal towns. A prevailing frost-free microclimate allows farmers to produce avocados, mangoes, custard apples (*chirimoyas*) and other exotic fruits – all of which you will see on sale at stalls by the roadside.

The coast's largest town is Motril, once centre of a sugar-cane refining industry, but it is not of much interest to the casual visitor. A few headlands round to the west is the large resort of Almuñécar, which is believed to have been founded by the Phoenicians and is now overrun by foreign tourists. The best beach on the coast is that of **La Herradura** (between Almuñécar and Nerja), which is a famously good place for scuba diving (you can take a trial plunge with the dive school at Marina del Este).

The prettiest place on the Tropical Coast, however, is Salobreña, a compact mass of white houses clambering over a great rock

THE SIGH OF THE MOOR

The last, hapless Muslim king of Granada, Muhammad XI, universally known as Boabdil, didn't have much choice in the end but to hand over the city he loved to the Catholic Monarchs on the best terms of surrender he could manage. It was only a matter of time before the Christians moved in, but at least the capitulations he signed in the nearby town of Santa Fe left him with a shred of dignity. The victors entered Granada on 2 January 1492 while Boabdil and his entourage left by the back door, going into exile in the nearby Alpujarras. A much-repeated story has it that Boabdil was heading south across the last low pass from which it was possible to see the city and he began to cry. His mother admonished him with the words, 'That's right: cry like a child over that which you couldn't defend as a man.' The pass, on the motorway towards the coast, has been known ever since as the Suspiro del Moro, or the Moor's Sigh.

◗ *Salobreña and its impressive Arab castle perched on a hill*

set back from the sea. Climb the maze of steep streets, steps and narrow alleys and you will reach a well-preserved **Arab castle** from which there are great views.

Guadix

Across the pass of Puerto de la Mora (1,390 m/4,560 ft) from Granada, heading east on the motorway towards Murcia and Almería, you descend into an ancient lake bed in which stands the curious town of Guadix. This has a group of handsome monuments in the centre, but no one comes to see them. What holds most

⬤ *Cool and comfortable cave homes in Guadix*

fascination is the **Barriada de las Cuevas**, a suburb of mud-hills drilled with innumerable cave homes – a much larger troglodyte community than Granada's Sacromonte. About 3,000 people live underground here, some in surprising luxury, and caves are sought after and traded just as houses and flats would be elsewhere. Several caves have been turned into cosy and comfortable hotels.

RETAIL THERAPY

Albayalde If the splendour of the Alhambra's decoration has left you feeling you'd like to make some improvements at home, you can always order a set of reproduction Moorish tiles at this shop outside Órgiva. ⓐ Cortijo del Cura, Órgiva, Alpujarras (near Hotel Taray) ⓣ (958) 785 199 ⓦ www.albayalde.eu ⓛ 10.00–18.30 Mon–Fri, by appointment only Sat & Sun

TAKING A BREAK

El Chambao de Joaquín ££ It looks like a mere hut near the end of La Herradura beach, but this is a cunningly sophisticated place that may cater largely for foreign tourists but is still a great choice for fish and seafood. At weekends, giant paellas are prepared. ⓐ Paseo de Andrés Segoiva 2, La Herradura beach, Almuñécar ⓣ (958) 640 044 ⓦ www.elchambaodejoaquin.com ⓛ 10.00–24.00 daily (Mar–Oct), 10.00–24.00 Wed–Mon (Nov–Feb)

El Peñón ££ Head for Salobreña beach and you won't be able to miss this restaurant that is affixed to the side of a rock, with a delightful shaded terrace over the water. The fish and seafood couldn't be fresher and you can often watch it being grilled on spits in the traditional way over an open fire. ⓐ Paseo Marítimo, Playa del Peñón, Salobreña ⓣ (958) 610 538 ⓦ www.elpenon.es ⓛ 12.30–17.00, 19.30–24.00 Tues–Sat

AFTER DARK

Teide £ Good salads and local food in this restaurant in the Barranco de Poqueira. ⓐ Carretera 2, Bubión ⓣ (958) 763 037 ⓛ 13.30–16.00, 20.00–22.30 Wed–Mon

Mesón Poqueira ££ A good place to sample Alpujarreño cooking. ⓐ Calle del Doctor Castilla 5, Capileira ⓣ (958) 763 048 ⓦ www.hotelpoqueira.com ⓛ 13.30–16.00, 20.30–22.30 Tues–Sun

ACCOMMODATION

Alcazaba de Busquístar ££ You'd be forgiven for thinking that this was another Alpujarran village because it has been built to create that illusion, even with its own church tower. Most rooms have a fireplace or wood-burning stove. ⓐ Carretera Órgiva, Láujar, Km 37, Busquístar ⓣ (958) 858 687 ⓦ www.alcazabadebusquistar.com

Almuñécar Playa ££ A large chain hotel that, as its name states, is right on Almuñécar beach and perfectly placed for exploring the town. There is a buffet restaurant and a swimming pool. ⓐ Paseo San Cristóbal, Almuñécar ⓣ (958) 639 450 ⓦ www.playasenator.com

Taray ££ This 'hacienda-style' hotel could serve as a base for visiting both the Alpujarras and Granada. It's also a good place if you just want to have lunch in relaxing surroundings. The gardens are planted with orange, lemon and pomegranate trees and there are tanks of trout on-site to supply the restaurant menu. ⓐ On the road out of Órgiva going towards Torvizcón ⓣ (958) 784 525 ⓦ www.hoteltaray.com

⏵ *A Granada postbox*

EXTRANJERO

PRACTICAL
information

Directory

GETTING THERE

By air

Granada airport receives mainly domestic flights, but it does receive a few international flights, notably those operated by Iberia, Spain's national carrier. Málaga airport offers much more choice. Flying time from Britain is around two and a half hours. For details of getting from the airport to the city centre see page 48.

Iberia Flights from the UK, most European and many other major airports. They, or their subsidiaries, operate domestic flights within Spain. ❶ (902) 400 500; in UK (0870) 609 050; office in Granada (958) 245 237 Ⓦ www.iberia.com

Many people are aware that air travel emits CO_2, which contributes to climate change. You may be interested in the possibility of lessening the environmental impact of your flight through the charity **Climate Care** (Ⓦ www.jpmorgan climatecare.com), which offsets your CO_2 by funding environmental projects around the world.

By rail

Mainline and local trains are operated by the national company **RENFE** (Red Nacional de Ferrocarriles Españoles ❶ (902) 240 202 Ⓦ www.renfe.es). Andalucía has a patchy railway network. The train is a convenient way to get to Granada from Madrid, Seville, Almería and Algeciras, but not from Córdoba and Málaga. The journey time from Madrid is about five hours. To plan a rail trip from the UK to Spain, it's best to go through an international agent such as **Rail Europe** (ⓐ 1 Lower Regent Street, London ☎ (08448) 484 064 ⓦ www.raileurope.co.uk). It takes about two days non-stop to get to Granada from London by rail.

The monthly *Thomas Cook European Rail Timetable* has up-to-date schedules for European international and national train services. **Thomas Cook European Rail Timetable** ☎ (UK) (01733) 416477; (USA) 1 800 322 3834 ⓦ www.thomascookpublishing.com

By road

From any of the French Channel ports, head south to Biarritz and cross the frontier at the western end of the Pyrenees (between Hendaye and Irún) to reach San Sebastián. Turn inland for Vitoria-Gasteiz and pick up the NI motorway for Madrid at Burgos. Madrid's orbital motorways take some navigating. The best policy is to go around Madrid to the east on the M40 following signs first for Zaragoza (but don't turn off for that city), then Valencia, then Córdoba. If you're lucky, you'll find yourself heading due south on the NIV motorway through La Mancha (past Aranjuez) and eventually through the spectacular pass of Despeñaperros into Andalucía. At Bailén turn off on to the N323 motorway, which skirts past Jaén to reach Granada.

Alternatively, to save driving through France, take a ferry from Portsmouth to Bilbao or Plymouth to Santander (crossing 24–30 hours) and drive south to Burgos and thence to Madrid.

Driving around the centre of Granada may take some getting used to and is best avoided in favour of walking and public transport. Parking can be both difficult and expensive and some people choose to double-park, which makes the traffic problem worse.

Spain drives on the right and its highway code is similar to that of other European countries, with internationally recognisable traffic signs. The police can issue on-the-spot fines for traffic offences and being a foreigner does not give you exemption. Seat belts are obligatory and children under 12 should travel in the back. Speed limits are 120 km/h (74 mph) on motorways, 100 km/h (62 mph) on roads and 50 km/h (31 mph) in built-up areas. It is forbidden to drive under the influence of alcohol. Most national driving licences are valid, but it is advisable to have an International Driving Permit if your licence is from outside the EU. In your car you must carry a red warning triangle and a reflective jacket in the passenger compartment to wear in

TRAVEL INSURANCE

Although EU citizenship gives you basic health cover in Spain, it is advisable to take out personal travel insurance as well. This can be obtained from your travel agent, airline operator or any insurance company. Make sure it gives adequate cover not only for medical expenses but also for loss or theft of possessions, personal liability and repatriation in an emergency. If you are going to Spain by car, ask your insurer for a green card and check with them on the cover you will need for damage, loss or theft of the vehicle and for legal costs in the event of an accident. If you hire a car, you will be asked whether you want to pay extra for collision insurance. You may already be covered for this by your normal UK car insurance.

case of roadside emergency. Petrol (*gasolina*) is available as *sin plomo* (unleaded) and *gasoil* (diesel).

When hiring a car you will be asked to show your passport and an EU or International Driving Permit. All the major car hire companies have offices in Granada and rates are competitive, but you can usually get the best deal by reserving a car from home at the same time as making a flight booking.

Avis ⓣ (958) 446 455 ⓦ www.avis.es
Hertz ⓣ (902) 402 405 ⓦ www.hertz.es

ENTRY FORMALITIES

Most visitors, including citizens of all EU countries, the USA, Canada, Australia and New Zealand, require only a valid passport to enter Spain. Visitors from South Africa must have a visa. There is no restriction on what items you may bring in with you as a tourist, but you'll find almost everything you need locally. In Spain you are obliged by law to carry your passport with you at all times, in case the police ask for identification.

MONEY

The Spanish currency is the euro. It is divided into 100 cents. There are coins of 1 and 2 euros and of 1, 2, 5, 10, 20 and 50 cents. The notes are of 5, 10, 20, 50 and 100 euros.

Banks are generally open only in the morning, 09.00–13.30 Monday to Friday, but there are many cash machines in Granada where you can get money out with a debit/credit card. Credit cards are accepted for payment almost everywhere except in smaller bars, shops and *pensiones*. Traveller's cheques can be cashed in banks and big hotels. Personal cheques are not accepted anywhere.

HEALTH, SAFETY & CRIME

British citizens – as all EU nationals – are entitled to free treatment from the Spanish social security system on production of a European Health Insurance Card (EHIC). Many travellers prefer to take out private medical insurance before travelling to Spain to give them greater choice of healthcare, should the worst happen. Like any European city, Granada has its share of petty crime, but most of it is opportunist and a few simple precautions will make sure you are not an easy target. Watch out for pickpockets in crowded places like markets and bars and keep your bag across your chest and in front of you. Leave valuables in a hotel safe and never leave anything on display in a parked car.

OPENING HOURS

Shops Usual opening hours are 09.00 or 10.00–13.30, 17.00–20.30 Monday to Saturday. In the summer, some shops open later in the afternoon, when the heat starts to die down, and stay open correspondingly later.

Department stores and other large shops open continuously 10.00–21.00. Shops are generally closed on Sunday except on special occasions such as the run-up to Christmas.

Post offices generally open 08.30–14.30 Monday to Friday, 09.30–13.00 Saturday. The main post office has longer opening hours (see page 134).

Banks usually open 09.00–13.30.

Offices (government and private business) open 09.00–14.00, 16.00–20.00 Monday to Friday. In summer, many offices work a reduced day, 08.00–15.00, and then close until the next morning.

Museums generally open 09.00–13.00, 16.00–20.00 Tuesday to Saturday and perhaps Sunday morning. They usually close on Monday, although there are exceptions.

Restaurants Mealtimes in Spain are later than in the rest of Europe. Breakfast in hotels is served 07.30–10.00. Lunch is 14.00–16.00 and dinner generally 21.00–23.00.

Entertainment Larger cinemas have several showings a day between 16.00 and 23.00. Some theatres offer two daily performances at 18.00 and 22.00. Bars for drinking and musical venues open 21.00–03.00 and discos 11.30–05.00 or 06.00.

TOILETS

Granada has few public toilets and the most convenient thing to do is go into a bar or café – in which case it is polite to buy a drink. There are public toilets in Plaza Bib-Rambla and along Paseo Violón. Another option is to use those in a department

● *Even Granada's toilets have the Moorish touch*

store like El Corte Inglés. There are several words for toilets in Spanish, the most common being *servicios*, *aseos* and *lavabos*.

CHILDREN

In Spain, children simply fit into ordinary life. There may not be many special facilities for them but this lack is more than made up for by a general tolerance and willingness to help. There are few attractions specifically for children in Granada and you might be best to spend a day or two in the city and then head for the beach. One particularly child-friendly place is the **Parque de las Ciencias** (ⓐ Avenida de la Ciencia ⓣ (958) 131 900 ⓦ www.parqueciencias.com ⓛ 10.00–19.00 Tues–Sat, 10.00–15.00 Sun ⓘ Admission charge), a sophisticated science museum with ten indoor galleries using the latest technology for its interactive exhibits and a large outdoor area, which includes a maze, butterfly house, olive oil mill and planetarium.

COMMUNICATIONS
Internet & Wi-Fi

There are several Internet cafés around the Plaza de la Universidad and Calle de Elvira. The tourist office can provide you with a list. Public Wi-Fi zones are also increasing all the time, and include numerous cafés and bars – just look for the distinctive Wi-Fi sticker on the window. The majority of mid-range hotels also provide Wi-Fi for their guests.

Media

The most popular European and US newspapers, including *International Herald Tribune*, *Financial Times* and *Daily Mail* (printed in Madrid), are available from newsstands (*quioscos de prensa*) in the centre of the city as well as at the airport. Many hotel rooms have satellite TV with programmes in English.

Phones

Local, national and international calls can be made from public phone booths (*cabinas*) in the street. They operate with coins or, increasingly, with cards alone. Instructions are written in several languages. Some call boxes take credit cards. Phonecards (*tarjetas telefónicas*) are on sale at tobacconists (*estancos*) and post offices.

TELEPHONING SPAIN

To make an international call dial 00 + the country code + the phone number. Spain's country code is 34. Granada's provincial area code, 958, must be dialled before all phone numbers, even for local calls.

TELEPHONING ABROAD

The country code for the UK is 44, for Ireland 353, for the USA and Canada 1, for Australia 61, for New Zealand 64 and for South Africa 27.

For international information ☎ 11825
For national information ☎ 11818

You can also find phone numbers at:
ⓦ www.paginasamarillas.es (yellow pages)
ⓦ www.paginasblancas.es (the normal phone book listing subscribers)

For any other information see the website of the national phone company, **Telefónica** (ⓦ www.telefonica.es).

You can also phone from *locutorios*, public telephone centres, which are quieter; pay at the counter when you have finished your call. Calls from a hotel room are more expensive than from phone boxes or *locutorios*.

Post

The main post office is on Puerta Real. It is open from 08.30 to 20.30 Monday to Friday and 09.30 to 14.00 on Saturday. If you just want stamps, you can buy them at tobacconists (*estancos*). To send a card or a letter up to 20 g to a country within the EU currently costs €0.64 and €0.78 to the rest of the world. After that, prices vary according to weight. Postboxes, marked *correos*, and both pillar boxes and holes-in-the-wall, are yellow. To send a telegram ☎ (902) 197 197

ELECTRICITY

Spain's electricity supply is 220 V, but you may find an anachronistic 125-V outlet occasionally in an older building, and for sensitive appliances like computers and mobile phones it is worth double-checking the voltage before plugging them in. All plugs in Spain have two round pins so electrical devices from the UK will only work with an adaptor. Visitors from North America require a transformer.

TRAVELLERS WITH DISABILITIES

Spain hasn't got many facilities for travellers with disabilities, but the situation is slowly changing. More information is available from **COCEMFE** (@ Calle Luis Cabrera 63, Madrid ☎ (917) 443 600 ⓦ www.cocemfe.es).

RADAR (Royal Association for Disability and Rehabilitation ☎ (020) 7250 3222 Ⓦ www.radar.org.uk) and **Holiday Care Service** (☎ (0845) 124 9971 Ⓦ www.holidaycare.org.uk) offer some information for disabled people visiting Spain.

TOURIST INFORMATION

Before travelling you can obtain general information from the **Spanish National Tourist Office** (ⓐ 79 New Cavendish Street, London W1W 6XB ☎ (020) 7486 8077 Ⓦ www.spain.info) by making a prior appointment.

For information about Andalucía in particular see Ⓦ www.andalucia.org. Another useful site, not official, is Ⓦ www.andalucia.com

The main tourist office in Granada is the **Centro Municipal de Recepción Turística** (ⓐ Calle Virgen Blanca 9 ☎ (902) 405 045 Ⓦ www.granadatur.com), but perhaps the most useful tourist information office is the one just off the top end of Plaza Nueva (ⓐ Calle Santa Ana 4 ☎ (958) 225 990). There are information points at Puerta Real, in the Alhambra and in Plaza Bib-Rambla.

For information about visiting Granada province there is a separate tourist office (ⓐ Plaza Mariana Pineda 10 ☎ (958) 247 128 Ⓦ www.turismodegranada.org).

BACKGROUND READING

Required reading for visiting Granada is *Tales of the Alhambra* by Washington Irving (see box, page 62). *South from Granada* by Gerald Brenan is another classic. The more recent *Driving Over Lemons* (and sequels) by Chris Stewart is a good introduction to the Alpujarras.

Emergencies

EMERGENCY NUMBERS

If you remember only one emergency number, make it ☎ 112, which will get you through to an operator whose job it is to put you through to the service you need. Emergency numbers are listed in telephone directories under *Servicios de Urgencias*.

Ambulance ☎ 112 **Policía Nacional** ☎ 091

Fire Brigade ☎ 080 **Policía Municipal** ☎ 092

MEDICAL SERVICES
Pharmacies

Minor health problems can be dealt with by a *farmacia*, a chemist's shop, indicated by a green cross. Out of hours, *farmacias de guardia* are open in every neighbourhood; you'll find addresses in the window of other *farmacias*. *Farmacias* should not be confused with *parafarmacias*, which sell non-prescription supplies and where staff may not be qualified.

Hospitals

The two hospitals closest to the centre are:

Hospital San Juan de Dios @ Calle San Juan de Dios 15
☎ (958) 020 000

Hospital Clínico Universitario San Cecilio @ Avenida Doctor Olóriz 16 ☎ (958) 023 259

POLICE

Spain effectively has three police forces. The Policía Municipal handles traffic problems and low-level policing. The Policía Nacional

EMERGENCY PHRASES

Help!	Fire!	Stop!
¡Socorro!	¡Fuego!	¡Stop!
¡Sawkoro!	*¡Fwegoh!*	*¡Stop!*

Call an ambulance/a doctor/the police/the fire service!
¡Llame a una ambulancia/un médico/la policía/a los bomberos!
¡Yiame a oona anboolanthea/oon meydico/la poleetheea/
a los bombehrohs!

deals with more serious crime. The paramilitary Guardia Civil, meanwhile, takes care of highway patrols and customs.

EMBASSIES & CONSULATES

Australia @ Calle de Federico Rubio 14, Seville ☎ (954) 220 971
🅦 www.embaustralia.es
Canada @ Plaza Malagueta 3, Málaga ☎ (952) 223 346
🅦 www.espana.gc.ca
Ireland @ Avenida de Jerez 46, Seville ☎ (954) 690 689
🅦 www.dfa.ie
New Zealand @ 3rd floor, Plaza de la Lealtad 2, Madrid
☎ (915) 230 226
South Africa @ Calle de Claudio Coello 91, Madrid ☎ (914) 363 780
🅦 www.dfa.gov.za
UK @ Urb Aljamar, block 7, No 145, Seville ☎ (954) 155 018
🅦 www.ukinspain.com
USA @ Plaza Nueva 8, Seville ☎ (954) 218 571 🅦 www.embusa.es

ACKNOWLEDGEMENTS

Thomas Cook Publishing wishes to thank NICHOLAS INMAN, to whom the copyright belongs, for the photographs in this book (except for the following images):

AISA/World Illustrated/Photoshot page 19; Dreamstime.com pages 7 (Dmitry Kutlayev), 68 (Canettistock), 83, 98 (Sborisov) & 112 (Domingo Leiva); PCL Travel pages 17, 30 & 79; World Pictures/Photoshot pages 5, 42, 59, 103, 109 & 121.

For CAMBRIDGE PUBLISHING MANAGEMENT LIMITED:
Project editor: Tom Lee
Layout: Trevor Double
Proofreaders: Jan McCann & Karolin Thomas

Send your thoughts to
books@thomascook.com

- **Found a great bar, club, shop or must-see sight that we don't feature?**
- **Like to tip us off about any information that needs a little updating?**
- **Want to tell us what you love about this handy little guidebook and more importantly how we can make it even handier?**

Then here's your chance to tell all! Send us ideas, discoveries and recommendations today and then look out for your valuable input in the next edition of this title.

Email the above address (stating the title) or write to:
pocket guides Series Editor, Thomas Cook Publishing, PO Box 227, Coningsby Road, Peterborough PE3 8SB, UK.

WHAT'S IN YOUR GUIDEBOOK?

Independent authors Impartial up-to-date information from our travel experts who meticulously source local knowledge.

Experience Thomas Cook's 165 years in the travel industry and guidebook publishing enriches every word with expertise you can trust.

Travel know-how Thomas Cook has thousands of staff working around the globe, all living and breathing travel.

Editors Travel-publishing professionals, pulling everything together to craft a perfect blend of words, pictures, maps and design.

You, the traveller We deliver a practical, no-nonsense approach to information, geared to how you really use it.

Useful phrases

English	Spanish	Approx pronunciation
BASICS		
Yes	Sí	*Sí*
No	No	*Noh*
Please	Por favor	*Por fabor*
Thank you	Gracias	*Grathias*
Hello	Hola	*Ola*
Goodbye	Adiós	*Adios*
Excuse me	Disculpe	*Diskoolpeh*
Sorry	Perdón	*Pairdohn*
That's okay	De acuerdo	*Dey acwerdo*
I don't speak Spanish	No hablo español	*Noh ablo espanyol*
Do you speak English?	¿Habla usted inglés?	*¿Abla oosteth eengless?*
Good morning	Buenos días	*Bwenos dee-as*
Good afternoon	Buenas tardes	*Bwenas tarrdess*
Good evening	Buenas noches	*Bwenas notchess*
Goodnight	Buenas noches	*Bwenas notchess*
My name is ...	Me llamo ...	*Meh yiamo ...*
NUMBERS		
One	Uno	*Oono*
Two	Dos	*Dos*
Three	Tres	*Tres*
Four	Cuatro	*Cwatro*
Five	Cinco	*Thinco*
Six	Seis	*Seys*
Seven	Siete	*Seeyetey*
Eight	Ocho	*Ocho*
Nine	Nueve	*Nwebeyh*
Ten	Diez	*Deeyeth*
Twenty	Veinte	*Beintey*
Fifty	Cincuenta	*Thincwenta*
One hundred	Cien	*Thien*
SIGNS & NOTICES		
Airport	Aeropuerto	*Aehropwerto*
Rail station	Estación de trenes	*Estatheeon dey trenes*
Platform	Vía	*Via*
Smoking/	Fumadores/	*Foomadores/*
Non-smoking	No fumadores	*No foomadores*
Toilets	Servicios	*Serbeetheeos*
Ladies/Gentlemen	Señoras/Caballeros	*Senyoras/Kabayeros*